Delivering Employability Skills
in the Lifelong Learning Sector

Delivering Employability Skills in the Lifelong Learning Sector

Ann Gravells

Learning Matters

First published in 2010 by Learning Matters Ltd.

British Library Cataloguing in Publication Data
A CIP record for this book is available from the British Library.

ISBN: 978 1 84445 295 8

Cover design by Topics – The Creative Partnership
Text design by Code 5
Project management by Deer Park Productions, Tavistock, Devon
Typeset by PDQ Typesetting Ltd, Newcastle under Lyme
Printed and bound in Great Britain by Cromwell Press Group, Trowbridge, Wiltshire

Learning Matters
33 Southernhay East
Exeter EX1 1NX
Tel: 01392 215560
info@learningmatters.co.uk
www.learningmatters.co.uk

CONTENTS

ACKNOWLEDGEMENTS

The author would like to thank the following for their support and encouragement whilst writing this book:

Jennifer Clark
Peter Frankish
Bob Gravells
Vic Grayson
Anne Metcalfe
Susan Simpson
Amy Thornton

The staff and learners of the teacher/training department at Bishop Burton College.

Philip Metcalfe and his staff at the Danesgate Skills Centre, York.

The author and publisher would like to thank Belbin Associates for permission to reproduce copyright material.

Every effort has been made to trace the copyright holders and to obtain their permission for the use of copyright material. The publisher and author will gladly receive any information enabling them to rectify any error or omission in subsequent editions.

AUTHOR STATEMENT

Ann Gravells is a lecturer in teacher training at Bishop Burton College in East Yorkshire. She has been teaching since 1983.

She is a consultant to City & Guilds for various projects as well as externally verifying the City & Guilds teacher training qualifications.

Ann holds a Masters in Educational Management, a PGCE, a Degree in Education, and a City & Guilds Medal of Excellence for teaching. She is the author of *Preparing to teach in the lifelong learning sector* and *Principles and practice of assessment in the lifelong learning sector*, co-author of *Planning and enabling learning in the lifelong learning sector* and *Equality and diversity in the lifelong learning sector*.

Ann is a Fellow of the Institute for Learning.

The author welcomes any comments from readers, please e-mail consult@anngravells.co.uk

Website – www.anngravells.co.uk

In this chapter you will learn about:

- the structure of the book and how to use it;
- delivering employability skills;
- Lifelong Learning professional teaching standards.

The structure of the book and how to use it

This book has been specifically written for anyone working towards the Certificate in Teaching in the Lifelong Learning Sector (CTLLS), or the Diploma in Teaching in the Lifelong Learning Sector (DTLLS). *Delivering employability skills* is an optional unit of CTLLS and DTLLS; however, the content is applicable to anyone delivering Employability programmes, or for continuing professional development (CPD). The book is designed to support the skills and knowledge you already have, and builds upon information in the companion books by Gravells (2008), *Preparing to teach in the lifelong learning sector*, and Gravells and Simpson (2008), *Planning and enabling learning in the lifelong learning sector*.

The book is structured in chapters which relate to the content of the optional unit. You can work logically through the book or just look up relevant aspects within the chapters.

There are activities to enable you to think about how you deliver employability skills, and examples to help you understand the subject.

At the end of each chapter is a reference and further information list, enabling you to research relevant topics, by using textbooks, publications and/or the internet.

Each chapter is cross referenced to the new overarching Lifelong Learning UK (LLUK) professional standards for teachers, tutors and trainers in the Lifelong Learning Sector (referenced by: S for *scope*, K for *knowledge* or P for *practice*).

Chapter 7 contains sample activities which you might like to carry out with your learners. These are available via the publisher's website, at www.learningmatters.co.uk.

The appendices contain the Delivering Employability Skills unit criteria and sample pro-formas you might wish to use. These are also available via the publisher's website to enable you to expand the amount of space needed for completion.

The index will help you quickly locate useful topics.

Delivering employability skills

Employability skills lie at the heart of the current Government's agenda for 14–19 year olds and adults at the time of writing. The reforms will raise the skills and qualification levels for young people and adults to world standards, as well as equipping learners with high quality skills for productive, sustainable employment and personal fulfilment. As a result, employers will have staff with the right skills for their businesses to succeed in a competitive global economy. Changes in technology are leading to changes in demand, in that employers are looking for more knowledgeable staff, with a broader range of workplace competencies and skills, which should complement academic or technical skills. Education and training in the United Kingdom are changing in line with this to ensure that every young person can have access to a high-quality, interesting and useful curriculum. This should help them achieve their potential, and progress to further and higher education and skilled employment. All learners should have the opportunity to increase their skills and knowledge, to achieve their full potential and social mobility.

> *The further education (FE) system plays a crucial role in securing wider Government ambitions of economic and social success through its development of the skills and talents of young people and adults.*
>
> *The FE Reform White Paper* Raising skills, improving life chances *and the Government White Paper* Raising expectations: enabling the system to deliver, *state that we will only sustain and improve our position as a leading world economy if the FE service is able to support the twin challenges of transforming 14–19 education and up-skilling the adult workforce.*
>
> (Department for Innovation, Universities and Skills (DIUS), 2008, p6)

You might be working with different age ranges and levels of experience in the world of work. Employability skills are a requirement for employment and are essential at all stages and levels of your learners' career development.

The types of learner you may encounter include young people or adults who are:

- facing barriers to employment – for example: disabled people; immigrants; older people; offenders and ex-offenders; those lacking basic skills such as literacy, or those with English as a second language; those without any qualifications or those who have been dependent upon benefits;

- going to be or have been made redundant;

- graduates;

- in employment but may face unemployment or reduced hours;

- in prison or a young offender institution;

- not in employment, education or training (NEET);

- more knowledgeable than yourself;

- pre-employment;

- returning to employment after a career break;

- school leavers;

- unemployed or between jobs and are seeking to enhance their employability or change careers.

You will need to appreciate the fact that some of your learners may be apprehensive about change, lack confidence or self esteem or have negative attitudes to employment due to their past experiences. Some may even be going through a grieving process if they have worked with the same people for many years and are now unemployed. You will need to be sympathetic to their circumstances. Finding out why they are attending, for example, due to redundancy, will help you to understand and support their individual needs. You will need to remain positive during an economic downturn to give your learners hope of obtaining and sustaining a suitable job. It could be that an organisation in your locality has closed down, making hundreds of people unemployed. This will have an effect on the local economy, and staff of all ages and experience will suddenly need help to get back into the labour market.

Where you deliver will have an impact upon *how* you deliver. For example, you may be in a training room or classroom every day. Alternatively, all your delivery might be in the workplace, or you may use a combination of the two. As you plan your delivery, further opportunities may become available, for example, setting up a realistic working environment (RWE) for learners to use, and using a blended learning approach incorporating information communication technology (ICT).

You will need to adapt your delivery style to suit the various needs and requirements of your learners, as well as the environment in which you will deliver, whilst following a suitable employability programme or syllabus. You might integrate aspects of employability skills within other programmes you deliver to give added value – for example, role play to demonstrate interview techniques. You might also deliver Citizenship, Settlement, English for Speakers of Other Languages (ESOL), or Personal and Social Development (PSD) programmes. There will be opportunities within all of these to deliver aspects of employability.

Functional Skills of English, maths and ICT will take over from Key Skills in 2010. When teaching, you should embed these within your delivery, to enable your learners to demonstrate their use in practical situations.

The current Key Skills are:

- communication;
- application of number;
- information and communication technology;
- working with others;
- improving own learning and performance;
- problem solving.

The first three are known as *hard skills*, the last three as *soft skills*. Both Key Skills and Functional Skills are important skills for learners to acquire as they are transferable to different situations and contexts. They can also improve employability prospects. Communication; working as a member of a team; problem solving and dealing with data and information are skills frequently specified by employers when recruiting staff.

You might teach Functional Skills or Key Skills as separate subjects or alongside an Employability qualification.

> *Functional skills allow individuals to work confidently, effectively and independently in life.*
>
> *To ensure that functional skills are readily available to the full range of learners, they are being offered as free-standing qualifications at Entry Level, Level 1 and Level 2 during the three-year functional skills pilot that began in September 2007.*
>
> *Functional skills will also be constituent qualifications of new Foundation, Higher and Advanced Diplomas.*
>
> (www.qca.org.uk/qca_6062.aspx)

If you are teaching the 14–19 Diplomas, your learners must achieve Level 1 functional skills for a Foundation Diploma, or Level 2 functional skills for the Higher (level 2) and Advanced (level 3) Diplomas.

Employability – the forward agenda (DfES, 2004) in England is a key document that sets out an employability development framework. This will address both short-term and sustainable employability. Emphasis is placed on the redesign of qualifications to ensure that learners are equipped with the foundation skills for employability, including embedding them in the 14–19 Diplomas.

Since Dearing (1997) recommended in his report on Higher Education that key skills development be a necessary outcome of all higher education programmes, national initiatives have made reference to the development of learners' employability skills. The *Employability skills programme* is an initiative jointly developed by the Department for Work and Pensions (DWP), Department for Innovation, Universities and Skills (DIUS), Jobcentre Plus, and the Learning and Skills Council (LSC) to help learners improve their skills. Funding may be available to deliver the programme through your local LSC, or from 2010 via its replacement The Skills Funding Agency (SFA). The SFA will deal with post-19 funding; the Young People's Learning Agency (YPLA) will fund 16–19 year olds and the National Apprenticeship Service (NAS) will fund apprenticeships.

The LSC believe that the further education system is uniquely placed to improve employability and skills, and to contribute to economic growth and social inclusion. Hence, relevant further education programmes are now identified and funded as *employer responsive*, for example, unit based qualifications.

Your organisation should have a strategy for delivering and assessing employability skills and the staff involved should be positive and proactive to ensure its success.

Depending upon the type of programme or qualification you are delivering, you might use different approaches, for example:

- a combination of methods (for example, a blended learning approach);
- a rolling programme with set start dates for each unit;
- delivering and assessing within a realistic working environment (RWE);
- delivering to different levels of learners within the same group;
- fast-track – taking into account learners' prior experience and knowledge;
- incorporating other qualifications (for example, literacy and numeracy);
- individualised learning programme with flexible attendance;
- integrated learning within an existing or new programme or qualification;
- integrating work placement with experience/voluntary work;
- self-study or distance/open/online learning;
- teacher-led – a discrete programme following a scheme of work to preset dates;
- utilising peer support, mentoring and networking opportunities;
- working with Higher Education Institutions (HEIs) for graduate-related employability programmes.

The approach you take may be dependent upon the numbers of learners, whether the programme is part time or full time, whether it is in a school, college or other environment, and whether funding can be obtained. The qualification you deliver could support other programmes, for example, Entry to Employment (E2E) or Train to Gain.

If learners undertake a work placement, or activities within a realistic working environment, it would be useful for them to complete an ongoing *work placement diary* (see Appendix 3). This will document the tasks they have undertaken, and their learning and experiences.

When delivering your sessions, you should always take into account equality and diversity, and health and safety aspects. You may need to carry out a risk assessment or liaise with others. Your sessions should be inclusive to all, and differentiate for any particular learner requirements. Making your sessions interesting and relevant, whilst inspiring, motivating and engaging your learners in the subject, will help them become independent and employable members of the workforce.

If you are passionate and enthusiastic about your subject, and can use interesting and memorable activities, you will help your learners' understanding, development and progression into employment.

The Leitch *Review of Skills* (2006) set out a clear agenda for change to move the UK towards becoming a world leader in skills by 2020.

> *In the 19th century, the UK had the natural resources, the labour force and the inspiration to lead the world into the Industrial Revolution. Today, we are witnessing a different type of revolution. For developed countries that cannot compete on natural resources and low labour costs, success demands a more service-led economy and high value-added industry.*
>
> (Leitch, 2006, p35)

To meet this target, the skills levels of people in employment will need to be raised. However, due to the changes in the economic climate, the number of people unemployed, and a reduction in government funding, this might not be attainable now. You will not only need to help raise the skills levels of your learners, but re-equip them for new careers, or encourage them to lower their sights or change direction if nothing is available in their chosen area. You will need to keep them optimistic about job prospects, help them overcome challenges, and gain experience and qualifications to obtain and sustain suitable employment.

Lifelong Learning professional teaching standards

In September 2007, a new set of professional standards came into effect for all new teachers in the Lifelong Learning Sector who deliver on government funded programmes in England.

The full standards encompass six domains:

A Professional Values and Practice;

B Learning and Teaching;

C Specialist Learning and Teaching;

D Planning for Learning;

E Assessment for Learning;

F Access and Progression.

The standards can be accessed via the Lifelong Learning UK (LLUK) website (www.lluk.org) or by using the shortcut: http://tinyurl.com/5mmg9s

The qualifications are based upon the Qualifications and Credit Framework (QCF) model, which has mandatory and optional units at different levels, and with different credit values. The units and credits can be built up to form relevant qualifications over time. Delivering Employability Skills is a 6-credit unit available at level 4 and can be found in Appendix 1.

The QCF is currently being phased in (England, Wales and Northern Ireland) and has nine levels; entry, plus one to eight (12 levels in Scotland). The framework helps learners to compare the requirements at each level, and to identify a suitable progression route.

Each unit has a credit value which represents ten hours, showing how much time it takes to complete a unit. There are three sizes of qualifications:

- Award (1 to 12 credits);
- Certificate (13 to 36 credits);
- Diploma (37 credits or more).

By looking at the title and level of a unit or qualification, learners will be able to see how difficult it is and how long it will take to complete. There are also *Entry* qualifications prior to level 1 known as Entry 1, Entry 2 and Entry 3.

A comparison of the levels to existing qualifications is:
- level 1 – GCSEs (grades D-G)
- level 2 – GCSEs (grade A*–C);
- level 3 – A levels;
- level 4 – foundation degree;
- level 5 – degree;
- level 6 – honours degree;
- level 7 – masters degree;
- level 8 – Doctor of Philosophy (PhD).

Further information regarding qualifications and levels can be found at the direct.gov website via the internet shortcut http://tinyurl.com/66ftqx

There are three teaching qualifications which fit into the new structure:
- Award in Preparing to Teach in the Lifelong Learning Sector (PTLLS) – a threshold licence to teach, with a credit value of 6, at levels 3 and 4;
- Certificate in Teaching in the Lifelong Learning Sector (CTLLS) with a credit value of 24, at levels 3 and 4, for *associate teachers*;
- Diploma in Teaching in the Lifelong Learning Sector (DTLLS) with a credit value of 120, at level 5 and above, for *full teachers*.

If you are an *associate teacher*, you will need to take PTLLS and CTLLS. If you are a *full teacher* you will need to take PTLLS and DTLLS or the Certificate in Education/ PGCE. All teachers must register with the Institute for Learning (IfL), the professional body for teachers, trainers, tutors and trainee teachers in the Learning and Skills Sector. Once registered, you must abide by their Code of Professional Practice. (Further details can be found via their website www.ifl.ac.uk)

For the purpose of the new teaching regulations, the IfL definitions of *associate* and *full* teacher apply whether you are working on a full time, part time, fractional, fixed term, temporary or agency basis:

Associate Teaching role means a teaching role that carries significantly less than the full range of teaching responsibilities and does not require the teacher to demonstrate an extensive range of knowledge, understanding and application of curriculum innovation or curriculum delivery strategies.

Full Teaching role means a teaching role that carries the full range of teaching responsibilities and requires the teacher to demonstrate an extensive range of knowledge, understanding and application of curriculum innovation or curriculum delivery strategies.

(Institute for Learning www.ifl.uk/about-ifl/faq/faq/category-two/
what-is-the-difference-between-aqtls)

The Delivering Employability Skills unit can be taken independently from any of the teaching qualifications, as evidence towards CPD. If you are taking the unit as part of a teaching qualification, you will need to meet level 4 requirements by showing an understanding of the relationship between theory and practice. You will also need to show evidence of research and reading, and also write in an accepted academic style using a referencing system, for example, Harvard. Maintaining a reflective learning journal, such as that in Appendix 8 will help you analyse significant events, evaluate your role and improve your practice.

Registering with the IfL, gaining the relevant qualification, and maintaining your CPD, will enable you to apply for your teaching *status*. This will be either: Associate Teaching Learning and Skills (ATLS) for associate teachers, or Qualified Teacher Learning and Skills (QTLS) for full teachers. This is a requirement under the Further Education Teachers' Qualifications (England) Regulations (2007).

Summary

In this chapter you have learnt about:

• the structure of the book and how to use it;

• delivering employability skills;

• Lifelong Learning professional teaching standards.

References and further information

Dearing, R (1997) *Higher education in the learning society*. National Committee of Inquiry into Higher Education (NCIHE) TD/TNC 2.281.

DfEE and DTI (2003) *21st century skills: realising our potential*. Department for Education and Employment and Department of Trade and Industry.

DfES (2004) *Employability – the forward agenda*. Education and Social Research Institute, Manchester Metropolitan University.

DfES Government White Paper (2005) *14–19 Education and skills*. London: HMSO.

DfES Government White Paper (2007) *Raising expectations: staying in education and training post-16*. London: HMSO.

DIUS (2008) *Further education colleges – models for success*. Department for Innovation, Universities and Skills.

Gravells, A (2008) *Preparing to teach in the lifelong learning sector* (3rd edn). Exeter: Learning Matters.

Gravells, A and Simpson, S (2008) *Planning and enabling learning in the lifelong learning sector*. Exeter: Learning Matters.

Lanning, J, Martin, R and Villeneuve-Smith, F (2008) *Employability skills examined: ten key messages from LSN's quest to understand employability skills*. London: Learning and Skills Network.

Leitch, S (2006) *Review of skills: prosperity for all in the global economy – world class skills*. London: HM Treasury.

LLUK (2006) *New overarching professional standards for teachers, tutors and trainers in the Lifelong Learning Sector*. London: Skills for Business.

Websites

14–19 Reform – www.dcsf.gov.uk/14-19

Employability Skills Programme – www.lsc.gov.uk/providers/employability/

Functional Skills – www.qca.org.uk/qca_6062.aspx

Further Education Teachers' Qualifications (England) Regulations (2007) – www.opsi.gov.uk/si/si2007/uksi_20072264_en_1

Institute for Learning – www.ifl.ac.uk

Key Skills – ww.qca.org.uk/qca_6444.aspx

Learning and Skills Council (LSC) – www.lsc.gov.uk

Lifelong Learning UK – www.lluk.org

Qualifications and Credit Framework – www.qca.org.uk/qca_8150.aspx

1 EMPLOYABILITY SKILLS AND EMPLOYMENT SKILLS

Introduction

In this chapter you will learn about:

- employability skills;
- employment skills;
- employability qualifications.

There are activities and examples to help you reflect on the above which will assist your understanding of employability skills and employment skills.

This chapter contributes towards the following scope (S), knowledge (K) and practice (P) aspects of the LLUK professional standards (A–F domains) for teachers, tutors and trainers in the Lifelong Learning Sector:

ASI, AS2;
AK2.2, AK4.2;
API.I, AP2.I, AP5.I;
BS2, BS4;
BK2.2, BK2.4, BK2.5;
BP2.5, BP3.5, BP4.I;
CSI, CS2, CS4;
CKI.I, CKI.2, CK3.3, CK3.4, CK4.2;
CPI.I, CPI.2, CP3.3, CP3.4, CP4.2;
FSI, FS3, FS4;
FKI.2, FK3.I, FK4.2;
FP3.I, FP4.2.

The standards can be accessed at:
www.lluk.org.uk/documents/professional_standards_for_itts_020107.pdf

Employability skills

Employability skills and employment skills could be considered the same; however, there are clear differences between them. Employability skills are the skills that make someone employable, for example, reliability and honesty. Employment skills are the skills required to perform a job effectively, for example, knowledge and experience of the vocational area along with literacy, numeracy and computing skills.

Employability skills can be grouped into knowledge, skills, attitudes and behaviour:

- knowledge – jargon, organisation specific, subject matter;

- skills – adaptable, hard working, organising, planning, resilient, trustworthy;

- attitudes – common sense, enthusiasm, initiative, integrity;

- behaviour – customer service, problem solving, self-management, team work, time management.

The Skills for Business Network (UK Skills) state: *Employability defines the knowledge, skills, attitudes and behaviours required by individuals to seek, obtain and sustain employment at all levels in the labour market* (www.employment-studies.co.uk/summary/summary.ph p?id=361). Possessing or developing these skills may not be enough. The report *Employability and employers: the missing piece of the jigsaw* (Tomkin and Hillage, 1999) states: *people also need the capability to exploit their assets, to market them and sell them* (www.employment-studies.co.uk/summary/summary.ph-p?id=361). Therefore, job search skills, career management, being adaptable to labour market developments and an economic climate, being realistic about opportunities, and a willingness to relocate are also required. Producing a professional looking curriculum vitae (CV), searching for and applying for jobs, and developing interview techniques are all necessary aspects of becoming employable.

According to Dr Peter Hawkins, (1999, p9) *to be employed is to be at risk, to be employable is to be secure.* He defined four groups of skills: people skills, self-reliance skills, generalist skills and specialist skills. Developing skills such as these will help your learners become more employable, and hopefully gain job security. In an economic climate, job security cannot be guaranteed. Years ago, the term *a job for life* was a reality. People would obtain employment after leaving school and stay with the same employer until retirement, often leaving with a good pension. Now, a job cannot be guaranteed and redundancy and short-term contracts are a regular occurrence. There are often more people applying for jobs than there are jobs available. People move to other areas of the country or abroad, and foreign workers come into this country looking for employment, creating competition for the jobs that are available. For economic reasons, many companies don't hold a reserve of labour; therefore, if a member of staff is absent, another member of staff will need to cover their job as well as carry out their own, or the job just won't get done. However, having skills which add value to a person's job role may help them to gain and sustain employment.

Examples of Hawkins's (ibid) four groups of skills are:

- people skills – communication, cultural awareness, team work, leadership;

- self-reliance skills – action planning, initiative, networking;

- generalist – commitment, flexibility, problem solving;

- specialist – organisation knowledge, technical skills and specific knowledge.

The following table shows some ways you could help encourage and develop these skills with your learners.

Table 1.1 Developing Hawkins's four groups of skills with learners

Skill groups	How learners could develop these skills
people skills	drama club; fundraising voluntary work; charity work; guide/scout/brownie/cub leader; member of an orchestra; networking; sport, for example, football, netball, hockey; working in a shop or restaurant.
self-reliance skills	amateur dramatics; debating society; Duke of Edinburgh Award; participating in competitive sport; playing publicly in a band; public speaking; Young Enterprise Award.
generalist skills	library/book clubs; member of local association, club or society; Mensa membership; project work.
specialist skills	European Computer Driving Licence (ECDL); first aid at work qualification; language interpretation; learning a new language; taking relevant qualifications; web page design; writing for a newspaper or magazine.

Activity

Look at table 1.1 above consider and note other opportunities which could develop the four skill groups. Hold discussions with your learners to help them list the skills they feel employers require and how they could develop them.

The Qualifications and Curriculum Authority (QCA) now known as QCDA, have developed the *Personal Learning and Thinking Skills (PLTS) Framework*, which, together with the functional skills of English, maths, and Information Communication Technology (ICT) covers the areas of competence that are most often demanded by employers. Integrating these skills into your delivery will provide your learners with a platform for employability and further learning. The skills are:

- team working;

- independent enquiry;

- self-management;

- reflective learning;

- effective participation;

- creative thinking.

The aim is to embed these skills across all areas of the curriculum for young people in secondary education and for adults. These skills fit well with employability skills, particularly in relation to team working and self-management.

If you are working with learners who are currently employed, or graduates seeking to develop their skills, you will need to help them realise their current skills as well as the skills they may be lacking. The definition of employability that underpins the work of the Higher Education Academy (HEA) is:

> A set of skills, knowledge and personal attributes that make an individual more likely to secure and be successful in their chosen occupation(s) to the benefit of themselves, the workforce, the community and the economy.
>
> (Yorke and Knight, 2006, p3)

This definition fits well for all ages of learners. However, you may be working with learners with different past experiences of employment and/or unemployment. Being unemployed can be demoralising and you may need to guide your learners towards different career opportunities. As a deliverer of employability skills, you will want your learners to gain employment, feel secure and become successful. You can do this by treating your learners as individuals and helping them realise their current skills, and future opportunities that could be open to them.

Example

Vijay is due to be made redundant in three months from a manufacturing organisation, which is closing down in a recession. He has worked there for 20 years on the production line, never having had any experience elsewhere. His employer has provided him with the opportunity to attend an Employability Skills programme. His teacher helped him make a list of his current skills (good timekeeper, honest, reliable, efficient), however, he has realised he is lacking in team work, making decisions, and creative thinking. He has never had the opportunity to take his driving test, which he can now. Vijay is being positive and treating his redundancy as a challenge to learn something new and use skills he hasn't had the opportunity to use previously.

Knight and Yorke (2003 p7) state: *employability skills refer to a set of achievements – skills, understandings and personal attributes – that make graduates more likely to gain employment and be successful in their chosen occupations, which benefit themselves, the community and the economy.* Being employable is therefore not just about having the skills to obtain a job, but to be successful within that job for the benefit of the organisation and others.

You may find you are delivering to highly qualified or experienced learners, perhaps graduates or people seeking alternative careers. According to McNair (2003), *successful graduates will need to have greater ownership of their employability skills and the confidence to cope with economic upheavals in order to identify and capitalise on career opportunities over a lifetime* (McNair, 2003, p2). You may therefore deliver *training programmes* rather than accredited qualifications to this type of learner. It could be that you are going to deliver an in-house training programme to employees facing redundancy. Their morale might be very low, therefore you will need to create a positive attitude, encourage mutual support and respect to help them develop the skills that will underpin their employability. Alternatively, you may be working with 14–19 year olds who have very little or no experience of the world of work. Always take into account your learners' prior skills and knowledge to help develop their employability skills.

Employment skills

Employment skills are the skills required to perform a job effectively, for example, knowledge and experience of the profession along with literacy, numeracy and computing skills. Employment skills include having relevant qualifications as well as the experience to do the job. If two people have been shortlisted for a job and one of them is qualified and experienced, but the other is only qualified, it is more than likely the person who has both will get the job. Professional knowledge, skills and experience only comes with many years of working and it is difficult for a person to gain the experience if they can't get a job.

You may be working with learners who are undertaking an apprenticeship programme and are mixing off-the-job learning with on-the-job training. This is a good way for them to put theory into practice and gain qualifications and experience at the same time. You might be delivering to younger learners who have never had the opportunity to gain any work experience, therefore you could arrange a work placement, or visits to various organisations. You might find it useful to find out what your organisational procedures are for arranging work experience opportunities. If you are working with adults who are considering a career change or facing redundancy, they will be experienced in their own profession but may need to start learning again for another profession. Besides gaining employability qualifications, your learners will need an academic or vocational qualification relevant to their chosen career or profession. You will need to find out what options are available to your learners.

You will need to possess good language, literacy, numeracy and ICT skills – having the skills yourself will enable you to develop them with your learners. If you feel you need to improve your own skills in these areas, don't be afraid to enrol on a relevant programme. You might be competent at using a computer, but not very good at using a keyboard. Learning to touch type is a way of increasing your speed and is a good skill for learners to possess if you can give them the opportunity. Literacy, numeracy and ICT skills are crucial skills as they are transferable between different jobs.

When delivering employability skills, you will need to embed aspects of functional skills within your subject.

Example

Shaun is delivering the Employability Skills Level 1 qualification to a group of 20 school leavers. He has decided to embed some aspects of functional skills within the Planning and Reviewing Learning unit. He has asked all his learners to access the internet, and locate a suitable learning styles test which they will then carry out (ICT). Once complete, they will look at their findings and discuss their differences with a partner, and write these down (English). They will then produce an action plan with clear targets and dates. If the learning styles test gave results in numbers, aspects of maths could also be embedded.

If you are not an expert at functional skills, you might need to liaise with other members of staff who could provide expertise, learning resources and materials until you gain in confidence.

At the time of writing, numeracy and literacy programmes are free to adult learners aged 16 plus in England through the *Get On* programme. If you work with adults who experience difficulties with literacy and numeracy skills, or would benefit from brushing up their skills, you could encourage them to enrol on a free programme by calling 0800 66 0800 or by visiting the *Get On* website at http://getondirect.gov.uk

In Scotland, the links are with adult literacy and numeracy and the core skills framework. In Northern Ireland the links are to the essential skills and key skills. In Wales, employability has clear links to basic skills and key skills as well as the Welsh Baccalaureate.

> *People with good maths and English skills are more likely to be in employment, with half of all jobs closed to people with skills below Level 1 (equivalent to a GCSE pass at grade D to G) and 98% of jobs closed to people with skills below Entry Level. In addition, better skills bring significant wage returns: research shows an earnings premium of at least 12% for good numeracy skills and 14% for good literacy skills. Previously published research shows that, on average, people with good basic skills can earn an additional £50,000 over their lifetime.*
>
> (DIUS, 2009)

The *Skills for life national needs and impact survey of literacy, numeracy and IT skills*, (2003), estimated that in England, 5.2 million adults aged 16–65 have literacy levels below Level 1 (broadly equivalent in difficulty to an English GCSE at grades D–G), and 6.8 million have numeracy skills below Entry Level 3 (the level expected of 11 year olds).

If your learners have access to the internet, they could use one of the many websites which offer free training, just ask them to search for *free online literacy* or *free online numeracy* etc. In the current marketplace and economic climate, the more skills a learner has the more likely they are to gain and hopefully sustain suitable employment.

Activity

Create your own list of employability skills and employment skills. Consider which you think are the five most important for each, given the current marketplace and economic climate. Discuss with a partner the advantages and disadvantages of those chosen and justify your reasons.

Your considerations should help you plan how to deliver and embed employability skills and employment skills with your learners. Being aware of the advantages and disadvantages will help you share realistic examples and anecdotes. You could carry out a similar activity with your learners to enable them to think about the skills, along with the advantages and disadvantages of each, and how they feel they can develop them.

Employability qualifications

Employability qualifications have been developed for the widest range of learners possible: young people and adults, those who are pre-employment, in employment, or between jobs. The qualifications are suitable for the 14–16, 16–19, and 19 plus age ranges, therefore are accessible to all learners. Employability programmes aim to:

- build self-esteem and self-awareness;
- develop learners' interpersonal skills, written and verbal communication skills and teamworking skills;
- develop learners' personal learning and thinking skills (PLTS);
- develop the attitudes and behaviours required in the workplace;
- empower learners to adapt to change, retrain and/or progress to further qualifications;
- enable learners to experience the reality of life in the workplace;
- encourage learners to take control of their direction to fulfil their potential;
- help learners to compete in and succeed in their chosen career;
- increase learners' employment prospects by raising their skills such as language, literacy, numeracy and ICT;
- meet the needs of learners who wish to obtain, gain and sustain employment;
- provide valuable accreditation of current skills and/or knowledge.

Employability qualifications can build upon skills already being taught or supervised in the learning environment or the workplace. The qualifications provide a solid grounding in generic employability and personal development skills, which will enable progression to work or employment and to further learning and/or other vocational qualifications. The programme or qualification you will be delivering may be called something other than employability, for example,

- Back to Work;

- Career Planning and Enterprise;

- Creative Techniques in Employability Skills;

- Employability and Personal Development;

- Entry to Employment;

- Personal and Social Development;

- Preparing for Employment;

- World of Work.

Most qualifications are on the new Qualifications and Credit Framework (QCF, or SQCF in Scotland), and the content of the units is agreed by all awarding bodies who offer them. The QCF removes *types* of qualifications and replaces them with standardised titles of Award, Certificate and Diploma which indicate *level*, *size* and *content*. If a learner does not achieve a full qualification, they will achieve *unit accreditation* for those units they have achieved. They can then add to these to achieve a relevant qualification later on. All learner achievements on the QCF will be held centrally, and each learner will be able to access their record electronically.

Example

Davinder commenced the Employability Skills qualification last September, and by November had successfully achieved two units towards a Level 1 Certificate. His family moved to another part of the country but due to financial circumstances, Davinder had to take a job. It wasn't a job he enjoyed and he desperately wanted to improve his knowledge and skills to gain better employment prospects. Davinder was soon able to attend a local college part time and continue with his qualification. He was able to prove his achievements by accessing the units he had obtained via the electronic database, enabling him to progress and complete the full Employability Skills qualification. As some of the units also occurred in other qualifications, he was able to see via the database what he needed to take to achieve these.

Learners will be issued with a unique learner number (ULN). This will enable them to access their achievements online and see which other qualifications their achievements contribute towards. Learners will be able to show their record to others, for example, potential employers.

The complexity of the content of a qualification defines its level, for example, an Award, Certificate or Diploma can be achieved from Entry Level up to Level 8 on the QCF depending upon its content (see the introductory chapter for examples of levels). The qualifications have mandatory and optional units at different levels with different credit values. The number of credits achieved defines the size of the qualification, not the level, for example:

- Award (1 to 12 credits);
- Certificate (13 to 36 credits);
- Diploma (37 credits or more).

The size can be calculated in terms of the time it takes a learner to achieve, for example, one credit equals ten *notional* learning hours. These notional hours are often a mixture of *contact hours* (time with a teacher) and *non-contact hours* (self study time). Some units available in one qualification will also be available in other qualifications, enabling learners to mix and match different units with different credit values to achieve their chosen qualification. There are *rules of combination* which state which units can or cannot be mixed or matched and at which level they must be achieved. The qualifications provide flexibility as your learner can choose units according to their level of ability, and their needs.

Activity

Obtain a copy of the syllabus for the qualification you are going to deliver. You may find all the levels are available within one syllabus, often known as a qualification handbook. This will usually be accessible via the awarding body website. Have a look at the content and see how it differs for all the units and levels. Ascertain which units are mandatory and which are optional. Do you think you will be able to offer all the optional units, or do you feel your own skills will need improving or updating beforehand?

Looking at the syllabus will help you understand the different levels and content which make up the qualification. If your qualification is on the QCF, the *learning outcomes* within the different levels will be similar; the difference will be in the *assessment criteria* for each level. This will be reflected in the language used and the depth of knowledge required to be demonstrated by your learner. QCA has produced *level descriptors* to reflect the abilities required for the achievement of different levels.

Example

Level 1 reflects the ability to use relevant knowledge, skills and procedures to complete routine tasks. It includes responsibility for completing tasks and procedures subject to direction or guidance.

Level 2 reflects the ability to select and use relevant knowledge, ideas, skills and procedures to complete well-defined tasks and address straightforward problems. It includes taking responsibility for completing tasks and procedures and exercising autonomy and judgement subject to overall direction or guidance.

QCA level descriptors can be accessed via: www.qca.org.uk/qca_20252.aspx

Tables 1.2 and 1.3 show the difference between an Entry Level 3 unit and a Level 1 unit for *Planning and reviewing learning*. Both have the same aim and a QCF credit value of 2. Although the credit value is the same, you can see the difference in the learning outcomes and assessment criteria which help define the levels. All units on the QCF are displayed in this way. The learning outcomes state what your learner *will do* (these help you define the content you will deliver). The assessment criteria state what your learner *can do*, these are the areas which must be individually demonstrated and evidenced.

Table 1.2 Entry Level 3 Unit 1: Planning and reviewing learning

Aim: To develop skills in planning and reviewing learning Credit value: 2	
Learning outcomes You will:	**Assessment criteria** You can:
1.1 Understand the skills and qualities needed for success in work and life	1.1.1 Identify the skills and qualities needed to achieve your goals
1.2 Identify your strengths and what you need to improve	1.2.1 Describe your strengths and what you need to improve 1.2.2 Agree what you are going to work on first
1.3 Identify your targets and plan how to meet them, with the person setting them	1.3.1 Say what your targets are 1.3.2 Say what you are going to do to meet the targets, and when 1.3.3 Identify deadlines for activities 1.3.4 Identify support to help meet targets
1.4 Follow your plan to help meet targets	1.4.1 Carry out activities to meet your targets 1.4.2 Review your progress with your supervisor 1.4.3 Identify targets that have been met

Entry Level and Level 1 qualifications are approved in England within the *Foundation Learning Tier* (FLT). The FLT is the description given to all qualification provision at Entry Level 1, Entry Level 2, Entry Level 3 and Level 1 within the QCF. The FLT supports a wide group of learners, including:

- those aged 14–19 unlikely to achieve their potential via the GCSE route;

- adults with basic skills gaps such as literacy or numeracy;

- young people/adults with learning difficulties.

The FLT curriculum is expected to be personalised within a qualification strategy that requires coverage of three curriculum areas:

- Personal and Social Development (PSD);

- functional skills (English, maths and ICT);

- vocational/subject-based (including employability skills).

Table 1.3 Level 1 Unit 1: Planning and reviewing learning

Aim: To develop skills in planning and reviewing learning Credit value: 2	
Learning outcomes You will:	**Assessment criteria** You can:
1.1 Confirm your targets and plan how to meet these, with the person setting them	1.1.1 Describe why targets are important 1.1.2 Make sure targets clearly show what you want to achieve 1.1.3 Identify clear action points and deadlines 1.1.4 Identify where to get the support you need, and arrangements for reviewing progress
1.2 Follow your plan to help meet targets and improve performance	1.2.1 Work through your action points to complete work on time 1.2.2 Describe different ways of learning and how you learn best 1.2.3 Use ways of learning suggested by your supervisor and make changes when needed to improve performance 1.2.4 Use support given by others to help meet your targets
1.3 Review your progress and achievements with an appropriate person	1.3.1 Say what you learned and how you learned 1.3.2 Say what has gone well and what has gone less well 1.3.3 Identify targets you have met and your achievements 1.3.4 Use feedback to help say what is needed to improve your performance

This mix of learning should increase potential achievement, progression and chances of employment. A key focus of the FLT is to establish set *progression pathways* for learners. Think of this as a *package of learning*, made up of a vocational or subject qualification; functional skills qualification; and PSD skills. There are four pathways available which intend to provide progression for learners to:

- a first full Level 2 qualification;
- skilled work or an apprenticeship;
- supported employment or independent living;
- a Foundation Diploma (Level 1) or GCSEs.

Further information regarding the FLT can be accessed via: www.qca.org.uk/ qca_8153.aspx

Your organisation will need to obtain approval from an awarding body before it can offer a qualification. The National Database of Accredited Qualifications (NDAQ) contains details of all qualifications that are accredited by the regulators of external qualifications in England (Ofqual), Wales (DCELLS) and Northern Ireland (CCEA). Scottish qualifications can also be viewed via the database. You can search details of all current and expired qualifications at www.accreditedqualifications.org.uk/index. aspx

As your learners progress through their chosen units, you will need to observe them in action. They will gather *evidence* or *proof* of their competence which you will need to assess. This evidence will demonstrate achievement of the *learning outcomes*. The *assessment criteria* will enable you to plan assessments appropriate to their competence. There could be opportunities to do this *holistically*, i.e. assessing several units at the same time. Your learners may have a *logbook* or *record book* provided by the awarding body which will list the learning outcomes and assessment criteria. This will help your learners plan and monitor their progress. Your learners can then write a number next to each of the criteria which relates to the piece of evidence put forward for assessment. Some awarding bodies will issue assignments for learners to complete, which ensure the assessment criteria will be met. One piece of evidence may cover several criteria and could be cross referenced many times. The evidence must be kept safe, for example, in a ring binder or wallet file.

Examples of learner evidence could include:

- action plan;
- annotated or highlighted text;
- application form;
- assessor feedback;
- assignments;
- audio/video recordings, for example, discussions/presentations/interviews;
- calculations and workings out;
- checklists;
- diary entries;
- e-mails;
- expenditure records/accounts;
- feedback records;
- Individual Learning Plan (ILP);
- interview preparation notes;
- job applications and advertisements;
- leaflets designed and produced;
- learner statements;
- letters – written or word processed;
- memos – written or word processed;
- models – hand made;
- notes;
- observation reports;
- photographs (authenticated);
- pictures/drawings;
- posters;
- presentations;
- products made;
- professional discussions;
- project plans;
- reports;
- research – notes and printouts;
- responses to questions;
- review records;
- role play (observed or recorded);
- tutorial records;
- work products;
- worksheets;
- witness statements.

To ensure learning has taken place and the outcomes met, you will need to assess your learners' evidence. You will be familiar with various methods of assessment by now, for example, observation and questioning. The syllabus may give you guidance as to which assessment methods to use. You will need to keep records of how your learners are progressing, and review their progress on a regular basis. Your learners' evidence and your assessment records will be internally verified within your organisation, and externally verified by an awarding body representative. You may also be inspected by representatives from Ofsted or other regulatory bodies. This ensures a system of quality assurance.

It will be your responsibility to deliver a suitable and appropriate programme to your learners to give them the skills they need to be employable.

Summary

In this chapter you have learnt about:

- employability skills;

- employment skills;

- employability qualifications.

References and further information

DIUS (2009) *News release (26/2009)* issued by COI News Distribution Service, 9 March 2009.

Hawkins, P (1999) *The art of building windmills – career tactics for the 21st century*. Graduate into Employment Unit.

Knight, P and Yorke, M (2003) *Employability in higher education*. Learning and Employability Series, ESECT:LTSN Generic Centre.

McNair, S (2003) *Employability in higher education*. University of Surrey: LTSN Generic Centre.

Stephen et al. (2000) *Integrating key skills in higher education: employability, transferable skills and Learning for Life*. Oxford: Routledge.

Tamkin, P and Hillage, J (1999) *Employability and employers: the missing piece of the jigsaw*. Report 361, Institute for Employment Studies.

Yorke, M and Knight, P (2006) *Embedding employability into the curriculum. Learning and Employability Series One*. York: Higher Education Academy.

Websites

Apprenticeships, Skills, Children and Learning Bill (2008–2009) – http://services.parliament.uk/bills/2008-09/apprenticeshipsskillschildrenand learning.html

CCEA – www.rewardinglearning.org.uk/

DCELLS – http://wales.gov.uk/about/departments/dcells/?lang=en

DIUS VQ reforms – www.dius.gov.uk/vqreform

Foundation Learning Tier (FLT) – www.qca.org.uk/qca_8153.aspx

Functional skills – www.qca.org.uk/qca_6062.aspx

Get On Maths and English free training – http://geton.direct.gov.uk/

Key skills – www.qca.org.uk/qca_6444.aspx

Learning and Skills Council – www.lsc.gov.uk

National Database of Accredited Qualifications (NDAQ) – www.accreditedqualifications.org.uk/index.aspx

Ofqual – www.ofqual.gov.uk/

Personal Learning and Thinking Skills – www.qca.org.uk/qca_10327.aspx

Qualifications and Credit Framework (QCF) – www.qca.org.uk/qca_8150.aspx

Qualifications and Curriculum Authority (QCA) – www.qca.org.uk

Qualifications and Curriculum Development Agency (QCDA) www.qcda.gov.uk

Scottish Qualifications Authority (SQA) www.sqa.org.uk

Skills for Life National Needs and Impact Survey of Literacy, Numeracy and IT Skills (2003) – www.dcsf.gov.uk/research/data/uploadfiles/RB490.pdf

2 PERSONAL QUALITIES, SKILLS AND COMPETENCIES NEEDED FOR EMPLOYABILITY SKILLS DELIVERY

Introduction

In this chapter you will learn about:

- personal qualities and skills;
- interpersonal and intrapersonal skills;
- feedback techniques.

There are activities and examples to help you reflect on the above which will assist your understanding of your own personal and communication skills.

This chapter contributes towards the following scope (S), knowledge (K) and practice (P) aspects of the LLUK professional standards (A–F domains) for teachers, tutors and trainers in the Lifelong Learning Sector:

ASI, AS2, AS4, AS5, AS7;
AK2.I, AK2.2, AK4.I, AK4.2, AK5.I, AK7.3;
API.I, AP2.I, AP2.2, AP4.I, AP4.2, AP5.2, AP7.I;
BS2, BS3, BS4;
BKI.2, BK2.I, BK2.2, BK2.3, BK3.I, BK3.2, BK4.I;
BPI.3, BP2.2, BP2.5, BP3.2;
CK2.I, CK4.2;
DP2.I;
ES4;
EKI.3, EK4.I, EK4.2;
EPI.3;
FSI, FS2;
FKI.I, FKI.2, FK2.I, FK4.I, FK4.2;
FPI.I, FPI.2, FP2.I, FP4.I, FP4.2.

The standards can be accessed at:
www.lluk.org.uk/documents/professional_standards_for_itts_020107.pdf

Personal qualities and skills

Job security is rare; therefore you need to demonstrate you have the qualities and skills to perform your job role effectively to sustain employment. You might need to retrain to keep up to date with changes in new technology or other relevant developments. The same applies to your learners – they need to ensure they possess or gain skills which are transferable to different employment opportunities. People tend not to stay in the same employment for their full working life; short-term or temporary contracts are becoming the norm. People must therefore be flexible in the qualities and skills they bring to the labour market. You might have had different working experiences which will enable you to relate to your learners. You might have been unemployed for a while, applied for several jobs, been interviewed but unsuccessful. All these experiences will help you demonstrate empathy towards your learners as you have experienced what they might be going through. Empathy is a skill that's difficult to learn if you haven't been there, you can only sympathise with others if you haven't had the experience yourself.

> The Leitch Review was established in December 2004 to consider the skills profile the UK should aim to achieve by 2020 in order to maximise growth, productivity and social justice. The UK must aim to improve its prosperity and fairness in a rapidly changing global economy. The Review has found that these changes are decisively increasing the importance of skills. Skills are an increasingly central driver of productivity, employment and fairness. The UK must achieve a world class skills base if it is to improve its prosperity and fairness in the new global economy.
>
> (Leitch, 2006, p27)

You can help your learners improve their skills through your deliveries. You may be delivering to a variety of learners, with different reasons for attending an employability programme. They may be demotivated or demoralised by circumstances beyond their control, for example, a recent redundancy or long-term unemployment. Your own personal qualities and skills can help motivate and enthuse your learners. Chapter 1 explained the many skills required for sustained employment; these skills also apply to you. You need to be passionate about your subject and committed to helping your learners achieve a suitable qualification and to obtain employment. Besides the skills to be effective at delivering employability, you may have certain qualities which make you the person you are, for example, being a good listener.

Activity

Make a list of the personal skills and qualities you feel you possess. Whilst doing this, consider your roles and responsibilities and the duties you will be performing. Analyse these and consider how you can develop them further, along with any you feel you need. You might like to identify your strengths, weaknesses, opportunities and threats – known as a SWOT analysis.

To effectively deliver employability programmes to your learners, you not only need suitable skills and qualities, but the competence and confidence to do this effectively. Being competent includes having appropriate skills, knowledge and experience, not only with the subject of employability, but with the concepts of delivering and assessing. Confidence comes from the experiences of using your skills and knowledge. If you are new to teaching, you may lack the confidence of delivering to learners, but be very confident in your subject. This could be due to past employment experiences, enabling you to use anecdotes with your learners. If you are currently delivering, you may be very confident with your learners, but not as confident with the delivery of the subject if you haven't taught an employment programme before. You will need to analyse what skills, qualities and competencies you have which will support your delivery of the subject. If you feel you lack any, find out what training or support opportunities are available for you either through your organisation, online or elsewhere.

You will need a variety of personal skills and qualities to effectively deliver employability programmes. You will also need various competences i.e. the abilities required to perform your role, which should be specifically stated within your job description.

Examples of skills, qualities and competences include:

- Skills:
  - adaptability;
  - organisation;
  - problem solving;
  - resilience.

- Qualities:
  - enthusiasm;
  - honesty;
  - integrity;
  - reliability.

- Competencies:
  - experience;
  - knowledge;
  - qualifications;
  - practice.

It is crucial you possess the skills, qualities and competencies knowledge you are expecting of your learners. They should be able to observe and emulate your passion and commitment towards being employed. If your learners have confidence in you, and you are able to thoroughly demonstrate your knowledge of employability, they will respect you as someone who can help them. You might like to carry out an activity with your learners to ascertain what they consider are the skills, qualities and competences required for their particular vocational area.

Other roles you will carry out include completing attendance records, reviews of progress, attending meetings, planning sessions and assessing progress. Responsibilities include a duty of care towards your learners, preparing the learning environment and referring learners to other points of contact if necessary. There will be boundaries within your role that you need to follow; but there is a point when your responsibility towards your learners stops. There will be times when you will want to help your learners, going beyond your responsibility towards them. If you have the time and capability, and feel this is not jeopardising your job role in any way, it should be fine. However, do be careful of becoming too personal with your learners as you could lose their respect and become involved with something inappropriate.

Activity

Think about where your boundaries lie in your current role. Do you have learners asking you for help with aspects you don't feel are your responsibility? If so, what would you do? Have you given your learners more support than you feel you should have, giving them an unfair disadvantage? How can you remain professional in your role?

You will need to get the balance right between supporting your learners towards their achievement and getting involved with any personal problems they may have. Knowing who to refer them to if you can't help them will enable them to seek expert advice, for example, if a learner has problems with finance. You might not be knowledgeable with all the information your learners expect, therefore having the names of people or agencies you can refer them to will help.

Understanding a little about your own personality will help you develop your personal qualities and skills. In the 1950s, a test was devised by cardiologists Friedman and Rosenham to identify patterns of behaviour considered to be a risk factor for coronary heart disease. This placed people as *Type A* or *Type B* and is still used today to analyse personalities. Type A individuals can be described as impatient, excessively time-conscious, insecure about their status, highly competitive, hostile and aggressive, and incapable of relaxation. They are often high achieving workaholics who multi-task, drive themselves with deadlines and are unhappy about the smallest of delays. Due to these characteristics, Type A individuals are often described as *stress junkies*. Type B individuals, in contrast, are described as patient, relaxed, and easy-going. There is also a Type AB mixed profile for people who cannot be clearly categorised.

There are other personality styles tests such as Myers Briggs (1995) and Keirsey (1978) which are based on the work of Carl Jung (1875–1961). Both involve a self-assessed personality questionnaire. Myers Briggs (ibid) focuses on how people think; whereas Keirsey (ibid) focuses on how people behave.

Myers Briggs (ibid) places people into eight categories:

- Introvert – territorial, need mental and physical space, pursue activities on their own, can feel lonely in a crowd, often work well with people;

- Extrovert – sociable, get lonely when not surrounded by others, life and soul of the party, need to be the centre of attention, get energy from being with others;

- Sensing – need things to be realistic, trust their experience and senses, down to earth, good at picking out details, often good doctors, nurses, policemen;

- iNtuitive – seeing things as wholes rather than details, trusts hunches, enjoying ideas, challenges and change, good inventors, innovators and pioneers;

- Thinking – making decisions based on principle, logic or objectivity, they like words such as analysis, principle, objective and firmness;

- Feeling – base decisions on their personal impact, they like words such as values, personal, persuasion, appreciation;

- Judging – liking things settled, orderly, planned and completed, they make lists and follow them, they get things moving, use systems and routines;

- Perceiving – does not like planning, preparing or cleaning up, are flexible and adaptable, delay making decisions hoping something better will turn up, are spontaneous, open minded and tolerant.

The letters I, E, S, N, T, F, J and P are used to denote each category. The benefits of the indicators enable you to have some knowledge of how people function, and enable you to realise that other people have aims and needs, feelings and values, etc. which may differ from your own.

Keirsey's (ibid) model has four main temperament groups:

- Artisan – concrete in communicating about goals and are flexible and accommodating about achieving them;

- Guardian – concrete in communicating about goals, logical, good at facilitating projects;

- Idealist – abstract in communicating, co-operative, good interpersonal skills;

- Rationalist – abstract in reasoning, utilitarian in achieving goals.

The temperament groups can be subdivided into character types, four for each temperament. There are also eight technical terms which are the same as Myers Briggs (ibid), for example, extrovert and introvert. The questions used will reveal a person's temperament and character type. You might like to carry out a personality styles test and encourage your learners to do so too. Reviewing your personality type should help you see aspects you might need to change, improve or develop, and can help you become more effective at delivering learning. Knowing people are of different types should help you realise how individuals act and react in different situations. The tests can also be used with your learners to enable them to see aspects of themselves that would contribute towards their employability.

Interpersonal and intrapersonal skills

A way of differentiating between interpersonal and intrapersonal skills is to regard interpersonal skills as *between people* and intrapersonal skills as *within a person*. Understanding and using these skills will help you develop a range of creative communication techniques appropriate to persuasive employability skills delivery.

Interpersonal skills are about the ability to recognise distinctions between other people, to know their faces and voices; to react appropriately to their needs; to understand their motives, feelings and moods and to appreciate such perspectives with sensitivity and empathy. Possessing interpersonal skills will help you develop personal and professional relationships.

Ways to improve interpersonal skills include:

- being a mentor to others;

- getting organised;

- meeting new people, at work, at social groups, clubs, meetings etc.;

- participating in workshops or seminars in interpersonal and communication skills;

- spending time each day practising active listening skills with friends, family, colleagues, etc.;

- starting a support/network group;

- striking up a conversation with people in public places.

Intrapersonal skills are about having the ability to be reflective and access your inner feelings. Having this ability will enable you to recognise and change your own behaviour, build upon your strengths and improve upon your weaknesses. This should result in quick developments and achievements as people have a strong ability to learn from past events and from others.

Ways to improve intrapersonal skills include:

- attending courses, e.g. Neuro Linguistic Programming,Transactional Analysis, Emotional Intelligence;

- creating a personal development plan;

- developing an interest or hobby;

- keeping a reflective learning journal;

- meditation, or quiet time alone to think and reflect;

- observing people who are great leaders, motivators, and positive thinkers;

- reading self-help books;

- setting short and long-term goals and following these through.

Howard Gardner (1993) defines intrapersonal intelligence as

> *sensitivity to our own feelings, our own wants and fears, our own personal histories,*
> *an awareness of our own strengths and weaknesses, plans and goals.*
>
> (Gardner, 1993, p239)

He is best known for his theory of Multiple Intelligences of which there are eight, interpersonal and intrapersonal being two of them. The other six are:

- Linguistic – the ability to use language to codify and remember information; to communicate, explain and convince.

- Logical – also known as mathematical intelligence. The capacity to perceive sequence, pattern and order; and to use these observations to explain, extrapolate and predict.

- Musical – the capacity to distinguish the whole realm of sound and in particular, to discern, appreciate and apply the various aspects of music (pitch, rhythm, timbre and mood), both separately and holistically.

- Naturalist – the ability to recognise, appreciate, and understand the natural world. It involves such capacities as species discernment and discrimination, the ability to recognise and classify various flora and fauna, and knowledge of and communion with the natural world.

- Physical – also called Kinaesthetic Intelligence. The ability to use one's body in highly differentiated and skilled ways, for both goal-oriented and expressive purposes. The capacity to exercise fine and gross motor control.

- Visual-spatial – the ability to accurately perceive the visual world and to re-create, manipulate and modify aspects of one's perceptions.

Individuals possess all of these intelligences; however, they are not all present in equal proportions (in extreme circumstances it may appear that an individual is severely lacking in one or more). The particular combination of intelligences and their relative strengths can form a profile that is unique to each individual. Some people are more intelligent than their peers; others appear superior at certain tasks, are more capable of manipulating information or more readily see the solutions to problems. Others are more expressive or more capable of learning. Being aware of differing intelligences within your learners, and in yourself will help you consider alternative ways of delivering your sessions to suit all your learners. Gardner's (ibid) eight intelligences have been debated and amended by many other theorists over time. They can be compared to various other theories of learning styles, for example Honey and Mumford's (1986) Activist, Pragmatist, Reflector and Theorist.

Neuro Linguistic Programming (NLP) is a model of interpersonal communication concerned with relationships and experiences. NLP is a way to increase self-awareness and to change your patterns of mental and emotional behaviour. Richard Bandler and John Grinder, the co-founders of NLP in the 1970s, claimed it would be instrumental in finding ways to help people have better, fuller and richer lives. They created the title to reflect a connection between neurological processes (neuro), language (linguistic) and behavioural patterns (programming) which have been learned through experience, and can be used to achieve specific goals. The model was based on how some very effective communicators were habitually using language to influence other people.

NLP training should help turn negative thoughts into positive thoughts. It provides the skills to define and achieve outcomes, along with a heightened awareness of the five senses.

NLP is an attitude which is an insatiable curiosity about human beings with a methodology that leaves behind it a trail of techniques.

Richard Bandler (co-creator of NLP)

The strategies, tools and techniques of NLP represent an opportunity unlike any other for the exploration of human functioning, or more precisely, that rare and valuable subset of human functioning known as genius.

John Grinder (co-creator of NLP)

NLP techniques can be used to:

● coach learners how to gain greater satisfaction from their contributions;

● enhance the skills of learners;

● improve own and others' performance;

● improve people's effectiveness, productivity and thereby profitability;

● set clear goals and define realistic strategies;

● understand and reduce stress and conflict.

NLP provides questions and patterns to make communication more clearly understood, for example, all thoughts and behaviours have a structure, and all structures can be re-programmed. Do you use jargon or clichés without thinking? Your learners might not understand what you are talking about, because you assume they already have the knowledge. To improve your communication and delivery skills, you can observe others who are skilled and experienced.

Activity

Arrange to observe an experienced colleague, preferably in your subject area, to watch how they interact with their learners. Observe how they communicate and deal with situations. If you can't carry out an observation, watch or listen to influential people on the television or radio. Ask yourself what it is about them that makes them successful. Can you emulate this in yourself, if so, how?

Language can be very confusing and easily misinterpreted. If you tell your learners not to do something, they will want to do the opposite as you have planted the situation in their mind. Language affects how both you and your learners think and respond to each other and enables you to devise strategies for dealing with challenges.

Example

Rosemary regularly struggles to hand work in on time. Her teacher, Alek, warns her she will not pass the qualification if she does not successfully complete the required outcomes. He has therefore planted negative thoughts into Rosemary's mind. What he should have done was give her some positive encouragement about how the achievement of the qualification will help her future prospects. He could also ask other learners to share with her how they ensure they complete their work on time.

Try and be positive and encouraging, rather than negative and complaining. When you understand the specific ways that your mind makes distinctions, then it is easier to make changes, to learn and to communicate effectively.

Emotional intelligence (EI) is a fairly recent behavioural model, given prominence in Daniel Goleman's book *Emotional intelligence* (1995); however, the model grows out of work originally begun in the 1970s and 1980s by Howard Gardner, Peter Salovey and John Mayer.

Goleman identified five domains of emotional intelligence:

- knowing your emotions;
- managing your emotions;
- motivating yourself;
- recognising and understanding other people's emotions;
- managing relationships, i.e. the emotions of others.

By developing emotional intelligence Goleman suggested that people can become more productive and successful at what they do, and help others to be more productive and successful too. He also suggested that the process and outcomes of developing emotional intelligence contain aspects which are known to reduce stress for individuals and organisations. This can help improve relationships, decrease conflict, and increase stability, continuity and harmony. The principles of EI provide a new way to understand and assess people's behaviour, attitudes, interpersonal skills, management styles and potential.

Emotional intelligence has been described as:

> *The ability to perceive emotions, to access and generate emotions so as to assist thought, to understand emotions and emotional knowledge, and to reflectively regulate emotions so as to promote emotional and intellectual growth.*
>
> (Mayer and Salovey, 1997, p5)

Becoming aware of your own emotions and how they can affect your personal situations will help you develop more fulfilling and professional relationships with your learners and colleagues.

The EI concept argues that the conventional measure of intelligence, IQ (Intelligence Quotient), is too narrow as there are wider areas of emotional intelligence that dictate and enable how successful people are. Despite possessing a high IQ rating, success does not automatically follow.

Activity

Think back to an experience you have recently had with a learner, where you were unhappy with the outcome. What went wrong and why? Now consider this experience using NLP and EI models, to enable a positive outcome should the situation arise again.

Demonstrating and evaluating your interpersonal and intrapersonal skills should help you effectively deal with situations. Passing on this knowledge to your learners will help them understand more about communication in the workplace.

Feedback techniques

Giving feedback to learners, whether verbal or written, can have a dramatic affect on their development. A lack of feedback, poor choice of words, or feedback given in the wrong time or place can be demoralising to your learner. You need to use an appropriate range of feedback methods which will enable you to give honest and constructive feedback in a variety of situations. Providing effective feedback to your learners can empower them through the development of their skills, confidence and self-esteem. Feedback can be formal, for example, a written document; or informal, for example, orally during the review process. Whichever method you choose you should not be ambiguous or vague. You need to be factual regarding the achievements towards the specific criteria or outcomes, and never just give your opinion unless you can back it up with relevant examples or facts.

Feedback should always be constructive and developmental to your learner, enabling them to know what they have done well (or not) and how they can improve or develop further. It should never just be an evaluative statement like 'well done', or 'that's great you've passed'. This doesn't tell your learner what was done well, or was great about it. Your learner will be pleased to know they have passed; however, they won't have anything to build upon for the future.

Descriptive feedback lets you describe *what* your learner has done, *how* they have achieved the outcomes and *what* they can do to progress further. It enables you to provide opportunities for your learner to make any adjustments or improvements to reach a particular standard.

Example

Cheryl, you have clearly met the criteria for achieving outcome 3.1.2 of unit three. You have obtained information from others using the telephone, which is one of the methods required. I liked the way you prepared notes in advance and practised the conversation beforehand. Your voice was clear and you had a good telephone manner. If you would like to aim for the higher level unit, you just need to demonstrate you can use more than one method of obtaining information.

This example shows how the feedback is descriptive and leaves the learner with a choice of what they can do to reach a higher level. A conversation could then take place as to other methods of communication. If a higher level wasn't an option, the assessor could have explained to Cheryl other techniques to use when making telephone calls. Try and engage your learner through interaction and discussion when giving feedback, making it a two-way process. If, for example, you are observing your learner and see them make a mistake, rather than stepping in to stop them, if it is safe let them continue, so that they can learn from it. When they finish, ask them how they feel they have done, which will give them the opportunity to state what they did wrong before you have to tell them. Consider your tone of voice and take into account your learner's non-verbal signals. Using your learner's name makes the feedback more personal, and making the feedback specific enables your learner to see what they need to do to improve.

Skinner (1968), a behaviourist theorist, argued that learners need to make regular active responses. These responses need immediate feedback with differential follow-ups; depending upon whether or not they were correct. Without immediate feedback, especially when the response is wrong, the learner will carry on making the mistake thinking they are right. They will then have to unlearn their response. Time can be wasted by learners unlearning their wrong responses instead of learning new behaviours. When designing any learning activities, consider how you can give immediate feedback to ensure correct learning has taken place. If you deliver one-to-one or in small groups, you should have opportunities to devote time to this. If you deliver to large groups you will need to plan in time for feedback throughout your session. A well designed learning environment should give you the opportunity to achieve this. Positive and negative reinforcement should encourage desired behaviour and discourage undesired behaviour.

There will be times when you have to give negative feedback. However, if this is done skilfully you can keep your learner motivated and enable them to see what they need to improve upon.

Example

Nashia, you did really well with the activity for criteria 3.1.2 of unit three by making a phone call to obtain information. However, I'm afraid you haven't achieved the outcome as you didn't obtain all the information required. Let's go over the requirements again and see how you can get it right next time.

In this example, the assessor explained what Nashia had done, but that she hadn't been successful, and then started a conversation as to how she could get it right next time. Using the word *however* instead of *but* sounds much better, as learners often don't listen to what is said after a negative word like *but*. Offering to go over the requirements again should help Nashia's understanding.

Activity

Think back to the last time you gave verbal feedback. What did you say? How did your learner react to you? Were you constructive and developmental by being descriptive, or just evaluative by saying very little? Next time you give feedback, ensure you are descriptive and specific. This should leave your learner clearly knowing what they have achieved and what they can do to improve.

Listening skills are also a part of giving feedback. If you are rushing your feedback, you might not hear any questions your learner asks. Learners need to be able to clarify the feedback you give, to ensure they know what they have achieved and still need to do. A change in behaviour occurs when learning has taken place. Giving effective feedback enables your learners to know what they have done right or need to change. As a result, their behaviour should continue to improve. This is particularly important in employment, to help identify any bad practice and work towards making improvements.

Questioning is also a skill you can use during feedback. Open questions such as those beginning with who, what, when, where, why and how enable you to obtain a detailed response rather than a closed question which may only elicit a *yes* or *no* response.

When questioning:

- allow enough time;
- avoid trick questions;
- be conscious of your dialect, pitch and tone;
- don't ask more than one question in the same sentence;
- involve all learners if in a group situation;
- try not to say *erm*, *yeah*, *OK*, *you know*, or *does that make sense* (the latter may only gain a *yes* response as learners feel that is what you want to hear):
- use eye contact;
- use learners' names;
- watch your learners' reactions.

When giving feedback in writing, it should always be written on the correct document, not just on your learner's work. If your learner loses the work you won't have a copy and you must maintain records to satisfy organisational and regulatory requirements. You can of course make developmental notes on your learner's work, for example, to correct spelling errors, or to make annotations showing you have marked it.

If you are writing feedback to be read by learners at a later date, you need to appreciate that how you *write* it may not be how they *read* it. It is easy for learners to interpret words or phrases in a different way to those intended; therefore, if you can, read the feedback to them at the time of returning their work. If you do not see your learners regularly, you could e-mail feedback to them. However, try not to get too personal — keep to the facts and be as constructive and positive as possible to retain their motivation. If you are giving individual verbal feedback, consider when and where you will do this, so as not to embarrass your learner in any way, and to allow enough time for questions. Giving feedback this way is also a good method of keeping in touch if you don't see your learners frequently, and also gives your learners the opportunity to communicate with you if necessary. Feedback can lose its impact if you leave it too long, and learners may think you are not interested in their progress.

Peer feedback can be useful to help develop and motivate learners. However, this should be managed carefully, as you may have some learners who might not get along and who might therefore use the opportunity to demoralise each other. You would need to give advice to your learners as to how to give peer feedback, such as starting with something positive, stating what could be improved, and finishing on a constructive note. If learner feedback is managed skilfully, you may find that some learners pay closer attention to the comments given to them by their peers than to the feedback that you yourself have given them.

The advantages of giving constructive and developmental feedback are:

- it creates opportunities for clarification and discussion;
- it emphasises progress rather than failure;
- it gives your learner confidence;
- it identifies further learning opportunities or any action required;
- it motivates your learner;
- your learner knows what they have achieved;
- your learner knows what they need to improve upon or change.

Feedback should always be adapted to the level of your learners. You won't help your learners if you are using higher-level words or jargon, when their level of understanding is lower. Conversely, you might come over as condescending if you use lower-level language with higher-level learners. You should also be aware of where you give the feedback, in case you are disrupted or are in a noisy environment.

Giving effective feedback is a skill that can be developed, and should lead to improved learner performance. Effective feedback can empower your learners through the development of their skills, confidence and self-esteem. Without feedback, learners will not know what they have achieved, or how they can progress.

Summary

In this chapter you have learnt about:

- personal qualities and skills;

- interpersonal and intrapersonal skills;

- feedback techniques.

References and further information

Gardner, H (1993) *Frames of mind: theory of multiple intelligences*. New York: Basic Books.

Goleman, D (1995) *Emotional intelligence*. London: Bloomsbury.

Leitch, S (2006) *Review of skills: prosperity for all in the global economy – world class skills*. London: HM Treasury.

Mayer, JD and Salovey, P (1997) What is emotional intelligence?, in Salovey, P and Sluyter, D *Emotional development and emotional intelligence: educational implications*. New York: Basic Books.

Myers, P and Briggs, I (1995) *Gifts differing: understanding personality type*. Palo Alto, CA: Davies-Black Publishing.

Skinner, BF (1968) *The technology of teaching*. New York: Appleton, Century and Crofts.

Websites

Association for Neuro Linguistic Programming – www.anlp.org

Carl Jung – www.cgjungpage.org/

Friedman and Rosenham Type A and Type B – http://changingminds.org/explanations/preferences/typea_typeb.htm

Honey and Mumford Learning Styles – www.peterhoney.com

Keirsey Temperament Theory – www.keirsey.com

Myers Briggs Type Indicator – www.myersbriggs.org

Introduction

In this chapter you will learn about:

- the learning cycle;
- learning techniques;
- support materials and resources.

There are activities and examples to help you reflect on the above which will assist your understanding of planning and delivering sessions.

This chapter contributes towards the following scope (S), knowledge (K) and practice (P) aspects of the LLUK professional standards (A–F domains) for teachers, tutors and trainers in the Lifelong Learning Sector:

ASI, AS2, AS5, AS7;
AKI.I, AK2.I, AK4.2, AK5.I, AK7.2;
BSI, BS2, BS3, BS4, BS5;
BKI.I, BKI.2, BKI.3, BK2.I, BK2.3, BK2.3, BKI.4, BK2.5, BK3.3, BK3.4, BK4.I, BK5.I, BK5.2;
BP2.I, BP2.2, BP2.3, BP2.4, BP2.5, BP2.6, BP3.2, BP3.3, BP3.5, BP4.I, BP5.I, BP5.2;
CK2.I, CK3.I, CK3.2;
CP2.I, CP3.I, CP3.2, CP3.5;
DS2;
DKI.I, DKI.2, DKI.3, DK2.I, DK2.2;
DPI.I, DPI.2, DPI.3; DP2.2, DP3.I;
ESI, ES2, ES3, ES4, ES5;
EKI.I, EK2.2, EK2.3, EK3.2, EK4.I, EK4.2, EK5.I, EK5.2, EK5.3;
EPI.I, EPI.2, EP2.I, EP2.2, EP2.3, EP3.I, EP3.2, EP4.I, EP4.2, EP5.I, EP5.2, EP5.5;
FKI.I;
FP2.I, FP3.I, FP4.I.

The standards can be accessed at:
www.lluk.org.uk/documents/professional_standards_for_itts_020107.pdf

The learning cycle

The learning cycle is a logical progression of events which should be followed for learning to be effective. This section will summarise the cycle; however, further information regarding all aspects of planning and delivering learning can be found in the companion book by Gravells and Simpson (2008) *Planning and enabling learning in the lifelong learning sector.* Further information regarding assessment and evaluation can be found in the companion book by Gravells (2009) *Principles and practice of assessment in the lifelong learning sector.*

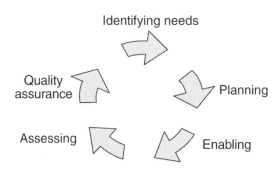

Figure 3.1. The learning cycle

Identifying needs is usually the starting point, enabling you to ascertain information regarding the programme you will deliver, and the learners you will deliver to. The needs of your organisation may have already been defined within the curriculum currently offered. You could ascertain what employment opportunities are available locally and create a suitable programme to meet these. You will need to obtain a relevant syllabus from an awarding body if you are offering an accredited qualification which may contain mandatory and optional units at different levels of learning. You will need to look at the content of the optional units to choose ones that meet the needs of your learners and the organisations within which they wish to work.

To ensure your learners take the units at a level appropriate to them, you will need to carry out an initial assessment to identify their needs. This should ascertain:

● any specific training needs, and any support and guidance they may require;

● any units they have already completed, or credit they have accumulated elsewhere;

● how the programme and qualification relates to their needs, for example optional units;

● the existing level of any specialist skills and knowledge;

● their career or job aspirations;

● their current language, literacy, numeracy, ICT skills;

● their learning styles;

● what they are good at or enjoy which could lead to employment.

The results of the initial assessment will enable you to agree an individual learning plan, action plan or contract with your learners. This should set out what your learner aims to achieve, how they will do this and by when. You should include long-term goals, short-term targets, personal goals and dates for reviewing progress. Regularly updating these plans will help motivate your learners by enabling them to see their achievements.

Coffield (2008) argues that you should take into account the whole *teaching and learning environment*, not just the individual differences in learners. It is therefore important to take the needs of your learners into account when planning and designing employability skills sessions. At first, your learners may not feel confident to inform you of any issues or concerns they may have. You will need to build up a rapport of trust with your learners and encourage them to let you know how you can help them. A careful question or conversation before or after a session when other learners are not around may facilitate this.

Example

Zarif had taken a group of unemployed adults for three sessions and noticed one learner, Kieran, had been reluctant to participate in the group discussions. At the end of the session, as Kieran was leaving, Zarif asked him if he had a minute for a chat. Kieran was apprehensive but came back in to the room. Zarif asked him how he could help him get involved with the group discussions so that he felt included in the sessions. It was at this point that Kieran confessed he had a slight stutter and had been bullied at school and college, which had seriously knocked his confidence. Zarif encouraged him to attend speech therapy sessions which gave Kieran the confidence to join in the group discussions.

Your learners should undertake an induction to ensure they fully understand the requirements of the programme, their responsibilities as a learner, and the responsibilities of your organisation.

Planning your programme includes preparing an appropriate scheme of work, session plans, resources and activities. Depending upon the time you have available you will need to consider the *product* versus *process* approach to your delivery. The product model focuses upon the content of a qualification, for example, the assignments a learner needs to pass to obtain certification, i.e. what *must* be delivered in order for the learner to pass. The process model focuses on the content of the course as well as other relevant knowledge and skills that the learner will benefit from. You may have learners who would like you to cover a particular topic which isn't in the syllabus, or hasn't been planned yet, but is relevant to their needs now. You could adapt your scheme of work to take account of this, enabling all learners to benefit.

The first session is crucial as your learners will need to know they are taking a programme that will help improve their job and career prospects. They will not want to waste their time with aspects they feel are irrelevant such as too much paperwork. Creating a good first impression is vital to help learner motivation and confidence. Some relevant subject matter should be delivered in the first session, don't just concentrate on introductions, rules and regulations and paperwork. Otherwise the session will purely be an induction to the programme and learners will not benefit by gaining new knowledge or skills. If you can't do this in the first session, you need to make it clear to your learners that the subject will begin during the second session, and that this first session is the induction to the programme.

Example

Using the pro-forma in Appendix 4, prepare a scheme of work for the delivery of your syllabus. Consider your target learners and their needs, and the requirements of the programme you will deliver. Plan what must be delivered to achieve the units, and what you could deliver to add value. Do be careful of dates when learners may not attend, for example, public or religious holidays. Plan to use innovative delivery techniques and resources. You could plan to use visiting speakers and specialist colleagues. Try and embed literacy, numeracy and ICT opportunities where possible. Work placements, realistic working environments (RWE) and role play could also be integrated.

Enabling learning is the third aspect of the learning cycle, and concerns the ways in which you will deliver your programme. This involves the use of various methods to suit your particular group, their learning styles and the qualification you are working towards. Always make sure your delivery and the activities you use are relevant and relate to the world of work, for example, using computers with up-to-date programs and equipment that is not outdated.

If you are delivering QCF units, the learning outcomes will be clearly stated and time will have been allocated to each unit based upon its credit value. The amount of contact and non-contact time should be specified in the syllabus. Do inform your learners in advance that they will need to carry out activities in their own time to support their learning, and help them plan what they will do with realistic target dates.

Assessment is the fourth part of the learning cycle; you will need to assess your learners' progress by using different methods and approaches. Assessment is a measure of learning at a given point in time; without assessment, you will not know how your learners are progressing. The syllabus will usually tell you which methods to use, for example, observation or assignments. Assessment types include formative (ongoing) and summative (at the end). You may need to design some assessment activities yourself, or use ones provided for you. All assessments should be valid, reliable, fair and ethical:

- valid – the assessment type is appropriate to the qualification being assessed;

- reliable – if the assessment is carried out again with similar learners, similar results will be achieved;

- fair – the assessment type is appropriate to all your learners at the required level, is inclusive, i.e. available to all, and also differentiates for any particular needs;

- ethical – the assessment takes into account confidentiality, integrity, safety and security.

Once you have assessed your learners' work, you will need to give individual oral and/ or written feedback and maintain appropriate records. You will need to manage the assessment process efficiently and effectively, not only for yourself but to demonstrate your commitment to your learners. You may need to liaise with others regarding the assessment process, for example, an internal verifier. The timing of assessments is important as this will enable a smooth transition throughout the learning process enabling learners to build upon their achievements.

Activity

Look at a unit you will deliver and read the assessment criteria. Design an innovative activity that could be used to assess your learners over a period of time. This could be an assignment that could take a few weeks to achieve and incorporate several learning outcomes. You could adapt one of the sample activities in Chapter 7 to ensure it meets your learners' needs and fulfils the qualification criteria.

Quality Assurance is the final part of the learning cycle and involves the use of assessment results, verifier reports, attendance, retention and achievement rates, and feedback from learners. This will form part of your organisation's quality assurance system which should ensure you have had a positive impact upon the experiences of your learners.

Throughout your role as a deliverer of employment skills, you will need to keep relevant records to satisfy your organisation, regulatory, funding and awarding body requirements.

Training techniques

You might be delivering formally in a classroom or training room, informally in the workplace, as part of a realistic working environment (RWE) and/or using a blended approach involving information communication technology (ICT). The techniques you employ with your learners should always be relevant to employability, and preferably relate to the context in which your learners wish to work.

> *All learning is concerned with changing behaviour, and ES [Employability Skills] training is no different . . . As a result of the training, however, the learner may become a more 'personable' individual, more self confident or less anxious when thrust into unfamiliar situations.*
>
> (Hind and Moss, 2005, p5)

Your ultimate aim should be to help your learners obtain suitable employment, as well as taking a relevant programme, or achieve a qualification that is tailored to their needs. You may be restricted to delivering the units of a qualification which attracts funding for your organisation; however, you should find ways to make these units interesting and relevant to your learners. Employment skills will not be developed instantly, they will take time depending upon the confidence and previous experiences of your learners. You may have a group of mixed ability learners, working towards different levels of a qualification, all with their own particular needs and requirements. You will need to develop the skills to multi-task with your learners, perhaps setting different activities to smaller groups or individuals within a particular setting. In this way, you can act as a facilitator, much like a supervisor at work, and create learning conditions similar to a working environment. Learners could agree their own targets for various tasks, work as teams to achieve them and evaluate the outcomes against the assessment criteria. Using this approach will mean you need to be flexible with your session planning and keep records of all learner progress. You should create a session plan for each session on your scheme of work. Each should have a logical structure with a beginning, middle and end.

The beginning of your session could commence with a *starter activity* to recap the previous session, perhaps in the form of a quiz. This allows time for the group to settle down and any latecomers to arrive. You could then introduce your aims for the session and what your learners will be working towards. It is useful to relate these to any learning outcomes and assessment criteria your learners will be taking. You could then introduce the tasks and activities to your group, discussing how these will be achieved in your setting, using realistic working conditions where possible.

The middle section of your session should concentrate on the relevant tasks and activities to be achieved. If you are facilitating a practical session, you could cause interruptions and move learners around to work with others to create situations that would arise at work. Wherever possible, relate your activities to normal workplace requirements, perhaps using timesheets, work progress records, changing deadlines and targets and holding meetings and discussions. To help differentiate for different levels of learners, create *extension* activities to challenge higher level learners further, and give them responsibilities such as supervising others.

It would be useful to engage with local employers and invite them to talk to your learners about the industry within which they work and any opportunities available with them. You could also arrange visits to local organisations to enable learners to see the type of work carried out.

The end of your session should include a recap of your aims, allowing yourself time to ask questions to check learner knowledge, and also for questions from your learners if they need to clarify anything with you. You should introduce the next session's aims so that your learners will know what to expect. You can set any homework or tasks that learners will need to complete in their own study time. If you have time you could hold a quiz to test knowledge gained from the session and create some competition within the group by offering a token as a prize to the winner. The tokens could be exchanged at the end of the programme for a trophy or an award. This could help keep learners motivated and make them keen to attend all your sessions. A final activity if you have time could be to ask each learner in turn *one thing they have learnt during the session that could be applied to employment*. This would help you see what they have learnt, and encourage them to speak in front of the group. It also helps them focus upon their learning and how they can relate it to employment.

You might not deliver from a pre-prepared session plan, but follow individual learning plans (ILP) geared to the needs of each of your learners. Whether you deliver formally, informally, from a session plan or ILP you should create an environment with a structure, activities and routines similar to employment but which is also conducive to learning.

It is important to vary the tasks and activities you use with your learners, not only to reach all their learning styles but to ensure that learning takes place. Using activities that relate to all the senses will help your learners' retention of skills and knowledge.

> *Studies show that over a period of three days, learning retention is as follows:*
> * *10% of what you read.*
> * *20% of what you hear.*
> * *30% of what you see.*
> * *50% of what you see and hear.*
> * *70% of what you say.*
> * *90% of what you say as you do.*
>
> (Pike, 1989)

Throughout your sessions, you should try wherever possible to give your learners the autonomy to achieve tasks as individuals or small groups. Fostering a climate of honesty, respect and trust will help them become responsible learners, and equip them with the skills for employment. Try not to talk down to, patronise, or be overly critical of your learners in any way otherwise they may lose their commitment and motivation to learn.

When planning and facilitating learning, you need to take into account the five principles of *Every Child Matters: Change for Children* (DfES, 2004) and incorporate aspects to support these within your sessions. In 2003, the Government published a green paper called *Every Child Matters* (ECM). Following the consultation, the Government published *Every Child Matters: Next Steps* (DfES, 2004), and passed the Children Act (2004), providing the legislative foundation for developing more effective and accessible services focused around the needs of children, young people and families.

> *A curriculum underpinned by Every Child Matters requires passionate and committed teaching that offers opportunities for open ended investigation, creativity, experimentation, teamwork and performance. It should also involve real experiences and activities.*
>
> (QCA, 2008, p2)

Whilst this relates to the well-being of children and young people from birth to age 19 (and vulnerable adults to age 25), the principles are relevant to learners of all ages. Whilst the C in the acronym ECM stands for *child,* it can easily stand for *citizen* and therefore be applicable to all your learners. Some organisations have adopted the term *Every Learner Matters* and applied the same principles.

Whatever their background or circumstances, learners should have the support they need to:

- be healthy;

- stay safe;

- enjoy and achieve;

- make a positive contribution;

- achieve economic well-being.

Table 3.1 on page 45, which you might like to add to, gives examples of how to promote these with your learners.

Get to know your learners as individuals. For example, each time you meet them find out something new about them such as their hobby, interest or aspirations for their future. If you have learners who are quiet and prefer not to speak in front of others you could devise an activity such as a *listening triangle*. Place your learners in groups of three and indicate who is A, B and C. A speaks, B asks questions and C takes notes and reports back to the full group (you can set the topic). This activity will enable all learners to take turns at each role, ensuring they listen to each other, contribute towards group discussions and gain in confidence.

Learners could work in small groups to find out information about the availability of employment within the area. You could devise a project for them to plan how they will do this, what they will aim to find out, and how they will report back to the main group. Time limits will need to be agreed and responsibilities defined. The project could include a variety of research activities such as visits to employers, online searches and telephone calls.

Activities learners could do individually include researching employment legislation and searching job sites. Learners could use a variety of means to obtain the information and prepare and deliver a presentation to their peers of their findings.

The activities you design should all relate to aspects of employment, either acting as fact-finding missions or incorporating the skills of being employed, such as teamwork, time management and communication. If you can inspire, engage and motivate your learners through interesting and meaningful activities, you will create a positive learning environment. If possible, individualising these activities towards the vocational area within which your learners wish to work may increase their employment opportunities.

Activity

Review the strengths and weaknesses of the training techniques and approaches you use at present to highlight the importance of creativity and innovation when delivering Employability programmes. Using the proforma in Appendix 5 prepare a session plan for your next delivery.

Table 3.1 Promoting the principles of ECM

being healthy	access to drinking water; areas for learners to practise their faith; availability of healthy food; discussions around mental health and personal issues; links with the community (e.g. care homes, libraries, nurseries, health centres, dentists); sport, exercise and fitness activities and events (indoor and outdoor).
staying safe	Citizenship Award; Duke of Edinburgh Award; health and safety training; introducing a buddy, mentor or peer support scheme; residential and field trips; visits to police, fire, ambulance stations.
enjoying and achieving	art and design activities; award ceremonies to celebrate learner achievement; contributing to community projects; taking the cycling proficiency test; taking the driving test; joining clubs and activities; longer term projects and investigations; music activities; peer discussion and debate; partaking in residential programmes; sport, fitness and outward bound programmes; using ICT; visits to museums, theatres, historical sites; working towards qualifications, e.g. ESOL, literacy, numeracy; taking youth awards.
making a positive contribution	encouraging learners to play an active part within your organisation, e.g. tidying areas, picking up litter, helping on reception, in the library, in the grounds, etc.; fundraising activities; group activities and team work; involvement in conservation and preservation; involving learners in decision making; role play; voluntary work; work experience.
achieving economic well-being	business and enterprise activities; financial accounting; fundraising activities; managing money; simulating a stockmarket challenge; inviting visiting speakers from various professions.

Whatever training techniques and approaches you use, you should aim to develop the skills, attitudes and behaviours that employers want to see in new recruits. You also need to ensure you are embracing aspects of equality and diversity, and health and safety. Try and make your sessions challenging and interesting, and embed English, mathematics and ICT throughout to help learners develop these skills.

Support materials and resources

All support materials, resources and activities you use should be relevant to the employability topic being taught and aimed at arousing an interest in your learners. As a result, motivation will be maintained and relevant learning will take place. You may be using resources designed by someone else and adapt these to suit your sessions or you could create them yourself. Usually, any resources you create as part of your job role become the property of your organisation. Do ensure you are being inclusive, i.e. representing all areas of your community and society. You can future proof your resources by making them inclusive from the start, for example, using larger text, printing handouts on coloured paper (for all learners rather than just those who are dyslexic), and using pictures and words that cover all categories of gender, age, disability, religion, etc. You may also need to differentiate for different levels of achievement. This is important as some units of the qualification you deliver may have the same content, but could be achieved at different levels. The assessment criteria will differentiate for the different levels. Learners taking a higher level will need to be challenged further and may need skills such as academic writing and referencing. All learners should be encouraged to use time management to plan activities to carry out in their own time which will support their learning and increase their employability. Examples of resources and activities you could use with your learners and those which they could carry out on their own are shown in Table 3.2 on page 47.

Your resources should be creative, innovative and engage your learners in a way that will encourage them to be proactive in their own learning. A well designed activity could include elements of teamwork, decision making, flexibility, problem solving and target setting – all skills that are required in employment. You may need to check any copyright restrictions if you are using resources created by someone else.

Activity

Look at a unit you will deliver, and think of a creative or innovative resource that you could design and use with your learners. Using the facilities available to you, create the resource, for example a handout, presentation or role play activity. Use it with your learners and evaluate how it went. What would you change about it and why?

You might find your activity went well with your learners, but it took you a lot of time to prepare. The more time you can devote to planning and preparing resources and activities that gain and maintain interest, the more your learners will benefit.

It would be useful to build up a store of support materials that your learners could refer to, manual and/or electronic. You could give your learners responsibility in developing a display area regarding various employment ideas based upon a theme, for example, catering, finance, retail, etc.

Examples include:

- business documents such as mission statements;
- handouts on various topics relating to employment, such as interview techniques, how to make a presentation, communication skills;
- information leaflets about setting up a business, becoming self employed, etc.;
- job advertisements, covering letters, CVs, application forms – blank and completed examples;
- leaflets on health and safety, equality and diversity, etc.;
- posters showing job search activities and lists of job search websites;
- sample letters to employers;
- study skills activities, such as Harvard referencing;
- video/DVD recordings, for example, job interviews, skills for particular vocations.

Having a store of resources will prove invaluable, for example, if you find you have spare time you could quickly access a useful activity, a leaflet or handout to help consolidate a topic.

Table 3.2 Examples of resources and activities

Tutor-centred	Learner-centred
• case studies; • competitions; • demonstrating interactive websites; • facilitating meetings which learners can take turns at chairing and taking minutes; • handouts to summarise points made during a session; • information about job share and franchise opportunities; • models and displays; • presentations of topics using a variety of visual aids; • puzzles and quizzes – useful for lower-level learners to test knowledge; • role play, for example, job interviews; • showing recordings of work activities and the right/wrong ways of doing certain tasks; • technology and ICT; • using telephone equipment to simulate and role play conversations; • worksheets – learners can fill in blanks whilst reading new information.	• completing job application forms (either as practice or real); • improving skills such as numeracy and ICT; • job search skills – online searches to relevant websites or by visiting Jobcentre Plus; • maintaining a diary of work experience or progress towards obtaining a job; • producing a curriculum vitae (CV); • researching companies and organisations in the area of employment sought – learning the jargon which is used; • researching how to be self employed, freelance or a limited company; • researching employment legislation; • studying various topics which contribute to employability such as body language, work ethics; • subscribing to and reading relevant journals, magazines, books, etc.; • using social networking sites to make relevant contacts; • viewing relevant internet clips; • writing a business plan; • writing letters of enquiry.

Activity

Create a bank of resources which you feel would be relevant to your delivery of employability skills. You might also like to designate an area of a room for a display of relevant leaflets and posters. You could involve your learners and create different displays relating to different employment opportunities.

There may be times when you feel you don't have the expertise to support your learners; therefore you will need to know who to refer them to. There may be staff within your organisation that could help, or you may need to direct your learners to agencies for aspects such as finance, health, relationships, drug or alcohol problems, community and religious groups.

The following are details of some of the many organisations that offer useful information and/or resources, along with their website addresses.

● Alliance of Sector Skills Councils – www.sscalliance.org

● Business Dynamics – a business education and enterprise charity. It runs programmes and seminars in schools and colleges to help bring business to life. www.businessdynamics.org.uk

● Business Link – free business advice and support service, available online and through local advisers. www.businesslink.gov.uk

● Careers advice – helpful advice on careers and learning. www.careersadvice.direct.gov.uk

● Centre for Education and Industry – a leading research centre for education and business collaboration, work related learning and vocational education. www.warwick.ac.uk/cei

● Connexions – an advice and support service to help young people aged 13–19 as they move towards adult and working life. www.connexions.gov.uk

● Department for Education and Skills 14–19 Gateway – provides information and resources in relation to the 14–19 curriculum for schools, colleges, work-based learning providers and employers. www.dfes.gov.uk/14-19

● Employment Information and Analysis – the Incomes Data Services is an independent research organisation providing information and analysis in key areas across the employment field such as: pay and reward; employment law; human resource policy and practice; diversity and pensions law and practice. www.incomesdata.co.uk

● Enterprise Zone – an online, interactive resource concerned with enterprise and work-related learning. www.edcoms.com

● Graded Qualifications Alliance (GQAL) – developed the UK's first performance based assessment system for measuring and validating social, emotional and employability skills. www.gqal.org.uk

- Jobcentre Plus – help and advice on job hunting. www.jobcentreplus.gov.uk

- Learning and Employability in Higher Education – a range of free guides useful for those who are reviewing or developing strategies for the enhancement of learner employability. www.heacademy.ac.uk/resources

- Learning and Skills Network (LSN) – provides a wide range of resources and services for schools, colleges and training providers. Programme teams which are particularly relevant to employability skills include; Vocational Learning Support Programme; Key Skills; Post 16-Citizenship and Support 4 Success. www.lsneducation.org.uk

- Learning and Skills Improvement Service – a World Class Skills (WCS) programme to forge links with employers to deliver effective training. www.lsis.org.uk

- myguide – a free, ready-made ICT skills tool to improve people's digital skills and confidence. It is designed to help the digitally excluded and novices, including those from disadvantaged groups. It has an impressive success rate, converting nine out of ten people into confident internet users. It has been developed with the support of the government and key partners. http://www.myguide.gov.uk/myguide/MyguideHome.do

- National Education Business Partnership – the national voice for education-business partnerships whose aim is to prepare young people for the world of work and adult life in general. It provides work experience and professional development placements; organises structured visits to the workplace; reciprocal visits by business; mentoring programmes and resources. www.nebpn.org/

- Next Step – a free friendly service that offers face-to-face help and support about training, learning and the world of work. www.direct.gov.uk/nextstep

- NIACE – The National Institute of Adult Continuing Education aims to encourage all adults to engage in learning of all kinds. Links to publications, events and member organisations. www.niace.org.uk

- Prince's Trust – a charity helping disadvantaged 14–30 year olds get their lives working through practical support including training, mentoring and financial assistance. www.princes-trust.org.uk

- Schools' Enterprise Education Network – a network of business and enterprise colleges providing support and continuing professional development for all secondary schools in England. www.schoolsnetwork.org.uk

- Sector Skills Development Agency (SSDA) – this website provides a list of all the Sector Skills Councils who have been charged to lead the skills and productivity drive in industry or business sectors recognised by employers. The Councils bring together employers, trade unions and professional bodies working with government to develop the skills that UK business needs. www.ssda.org.uk

- Skills for Life – resources developed by the Learning and Skills Improvement Service (LSIS) for ESOL, literacy, language and numeracy. www.excellencegateway.org.uk/sflcurriculum

- Teachernet – covers employer involvement in 14–19 education and training; GCSEs in vocational subjects; work-related learning; enterprise education for schools; and young apprenticeships. www.teachernet.gov.uk

- UK Commission for Employment and Skills (UKCES) – their aim is to raise prosperity and opportunity for people by helping to develop world-class employment and skills systems. www.ukces.org.uk

- Union Learn – help unions spread the lifelong learning message to working people. www.unionlearn.org.uk

- 14–19 Vocational Learning Support Programme (VLSP) – supports the delivery and implementation of applied GCSEs, A-levels and other vocational qualifications for 14–19 year olds. It does this through high quality training, networks, support, materials and resources for practitioners, learners and others. www.vocationallearning.org.uk

- Young Enterprise – a business and enterprise education charity offering a range of programmes, based on Learning by Doing, which bring volunteers from business into the learning environment. The aim of the programmes is to help build a better-motivated, educated, enterprising workforce, at the same time making a real difference to the lives and future potential of young people in their area. www.young-enterprise.org.uk

Summary

In this chapter you have learnt about:

- the learning cycle;

- training techniques;

- support materials and resources.

References and further information

Coffield, F (2008) *Just suppose teaching and learning became the first priority. . .* London: LSN.

DfES (2004) *Every Child Matters: change for children*. London: DfES 1110 2004.

DfES (2004) *Every Child Matters: next steps*. London: DfES 0240 2004.

Gravells, A (2009) *Principles and practice of assessment in the lifelong learning sector*. Exeter: Learning Matters.

Gravells, A and Simpson, S (2008) *Planning and enabling learning in the lifelong learning sector*. Exeter: Learning Matters.

Gravells, A and Simpson, S (2009) *Equality and diversity in the lifelong learning sector*. Exeter: Learning Matters.

Harvey, L, Locke, W and Morey, A (2002) *Enhancing employability, recognising diversity*. Universities UK: CSU.

Hind, D and Moss, S (2005) *Employability skills*. Houghton-le-Spring: Business Education Publishers.

Pike, RW (1989) *Creative training techniques handbook*. Minneapolis, MN: Lakewood Books.

QCA (2008) *Every Child Matters at the heart of the curriculum*. London: QCA/07/3317.

Reece, I and Walker, S (2007) *Teaching, training and learning* (6th edn). Sunderland: Business Education Publishers.

Websites

Every Child Matters – www.dcsf.gov.uk/everychildmatters

Learning styles – www.brainboxx.co.uk/A2_LEARNSTYLES/pages/learning styles.htm

4 THE TRAINING ENVIRONMENT AND PERSONAL PRESENTATION SKILLS

Introduction

In this chapter you will learn about:

- the training/realistic working environment;
- behaviour and motivation;
- dress and personal presentation.

There are activities and examples to help you reflect on the above which will assist your understanding of the training environment and personal presentation skills.

This chapter contributes towards the following scope (S), knowledge (K) and practice (P) aspects of the LLUK professional standards (A–F domains) for teachers, tutors and trainers in the Lifelong Learning Sector:

AS1, AS2, AS3, AS4, AS5, AS6;
AK1.1, AK2.1, AK2.2, AK3.1, AK4.1, AK4.2, AK4.3, AK5.1, AK5.2, AK6.1;
AP1.1, AP2.1, AP2.2, AP3.1, AP5.1, AP5.2, AP6.2;
BS1, BS2, BS3, BS4;
BK1.1, BK1.2, BK1.3, BK2.2, BK2.3, BK2.4, BK2.5, BK3.1, BK3.4, BK4.1, BK5.1, BK5.2;
BP1.1, BP1.2, BP1.3, BP2.1, BP2.2, BP2.3, BP2.4, BP2.5, BP3.1;
CS2, CS3, CS4;
CK1.1, CK1.2, CK2.1, CK3.1, CK3.2, CK3.5;
CP1.2, CP2.1, CP3.1, CP3.2, CP3.5;
DS1, DS2;
DK1.1, DK1.2, DK1.3, DK2.1;
DP1.1, DP1.2, DP1.3;
FS1, FS2;
FK1.1, FK1.2, FK4.1;
FP1.1, FP1.2, FP3.1, FP4.2.

The standards can be accessed at:
www.lluk.org.uk/documents/professional_standards_for_itts_20107.pdf

The training/realistic working environment

You may need to create an environment for your learners that, insofar as is possible reflects that of the workplace. Simulating working practices in surroundings and in an atmosphere which is as realistic as possible will enable your learners to gain an insight into work ethics and practices. A practical and purposeful environment can be a welcome option for learners who have become disengaged from employment, education and training. The impression you give is as important to your learners as the experience you give them. Depending upon where you are delivering, you will need to create suitable areas for the achievement of relevant tasks and activities. Creating a realistic working environment (RWE) within your organisation would be the ideal way to do this. Learners can carry out real tasks in a safe environment, which members of the public and/or staff can access. You will therefore act as a supervisor or manager to facilitate the session and ensure that it operates like a workplace. You can demonstrate relevant jobs to your learners then let them carry them out themselves, as if they were at work. Some will learn quicker than others and you may have to demonstrate the same topic several times. Giving your learners a handout to back up your demonstrations will give them something to refer to afterwards. This can be like referring to an instruction manual in the workplace. Try and create an atmosphere whereby your learners feel able to ask you questions, but can plan their own workload and become autonomous workers. If you are delivering in a specific vocational area, you should be experienced and/or qualified yourself enabling you to draw on your knowledge and skills to the benefit of your learners.

A RWE should offer facilities for learners to:

- actively carry out realistic and relevant work activities;
- be assessed at an appropriate level and time towards a relevant qualification;
- communicate effectively using different techniques in a variety of situations;
- control their own progress and development;
- gain the skills and experience they need for employment;
- have a clear sense of purpose and work in a professional atmosphere;
- have access to people, equipment and materials that would be found in employment;
- integrate English, mathematics and ICT in routine tasks and other relevant activities;
- plan, manage and complete realistic activities to meet deadlines and targets;
- solve problems in a variety of circumstances;
- use equipment and computer programs such as those in the working environment;
- work well as an individual as well as part of a team.

You might already be delivering in a RWE and have the resources and facilities you need; however, you will need to check that these are up to date and reflect the current working conditions in the vocational area. There may be other vocational RWEs in your organisation, or areas of your organisation where your learners could go for work experience. You will need to find out what is available and communicate with relevant people. If you have to create a RWE, you will need to research what you will need, perhaps by visiting local organisations and making useful contacts. You will need to recognise the needs of business as well as the needs of your learners to ensure a suitable match. The RWE should operate like an actual workplace with various demands, routines and interruptions that can take your learners outside their comfort zone. Opportunities should be taken wherever possible to inform your learners about the world of work and employers' expectations. You could create a *signing in and out system* to ensure learners are on time and don't abuse the time they take for a break. Alternatively you could operate a flexible working time arrangement, enabling learners who have other commitments to attend. You could set tasks for individuals and groups to complete within a certain time scale and nominate different learners in turn to supervise and report to you. You could give promotions to supervisory positions as a reward for work well done or achievements ahead of target dates. If you have a large group, it may be difficult to keep an eye on all the activities taking place, therefore learners acting as supervisors can help with this. You will need to develop skills of listening carefully to everything that is happening in the room, even when you are in a conversation. You need to remain in control and observe what is going on at all times. As soon as anything untoward happens you will need to deal with it before it gets out of hand. Although the area should be realistic to the workplace, it should also be an enjoyable space for learners to work and gain new skills and knowledge.

Examples of RWEs include:

- hair and beauty salon;

- office;

- practical skill areas such as: construction, horticulture, joinery, motor vehicle, plumbing, etc.;

- restaurant and kitchen/catering areas;

- retail, for example, setting up and operating a tuck shop or stationery shop.

A RWE can be used to accommodate all levels of learners who are working towards different qualifications and career aspirations. The facilities could be available Monday to Friday, evenings and/or weekends. They can be used by full time, part time, and day release learners as well as pupils from schools on experiential programmes. They could also be used to offer taster days for future learners. You might not deliver in the RWE on your own, but share the facilities with others at the same time or different times. Communication is the key to ensure the smooth running of the RWE.

Example

Paola had been asked to set up an office RWE within her college. The classroom she normally used was of a decent size enabling her to move the tables into several 'L' shapes to create an open plan office with computer workstations. A reception desk was created at the entrance to the room with a signing in/out book and a work in/out log. Each day, learners would sign in and carry out work allocated to them by the person whose turn it was to be a receptionist. Paola asked her learners to design a leaflet and poster to advertise their services. They offered various facilities such as photocopying, word processing, franking mail, internet research and desktop publishing. The RWE started by offering free services to the college staff. As the office became successful, they were able to begin charging for services to learners and external customers, and also to lengthen their opening hours. This created other opportunities for finance, budgeting, ordering resources, stock control, quality control and flexible working patterns.

In this example, learners acted as though they were going to work, carrying out allocated tasks and working to deadlines. Learners took turns at being the receptionist and higher-level learners supervised lower-level learners. During quiet periods, learners could carry out job search activities and assignments.

There will be times when you will need to cover theoretical subjects and the RWE may not be an appropriate setting for this. You could create an area within the RWE for formal delivery or use a classroom, meeting room or other appropriate area if available. You could use interactive technology and online forums, view clips via the internet, television recordings/DVDs/videos of relevant topics, and use practical demonstrations to support your delivery and bring it to life. Aspects you could cover besides those relating to the vocational subject include:

- business and workplace ethics;
- commercial awareness;
- dealing with difficult situations;
- enterprise and entrepreneurship;
- environment issues;
- equality and diversity;
- European developments and opportunities;
- finance and budgeting, tax and national insurance;
- health and safety;
- job search, application and interview skills;
- problem solving, decision making, negotiation, delegation and teamwork;
- project management;
- relevant legislation and regulations;

- self employment, creating a business plan, forming a company;

- spiritual, moral, ethical, social and cultural issues;

- the three sectors – public, private and voluntary.

Appropriate links should be made between theory and practice by applying the topics to realistic examples, and drawing upon your learners' experiences.

You will need to refer to the programme requirements to ascertain what topics you should deliver; you can then plan to cover other relevant topics as necessary. The Health and Safety at Work Act 1974 (HASAWA) makes health and safety everybody's responsibility, promotes safety awareness, and helps people work together to keep each other safe. You should ensure you are familiar with any legislation that affects your RWE. You might need to carry out risk assessments before letting your learners use specialist equipment, and maintain relevant records.

Activity

How could you transform your current area to reflect a RWE? If you can't acquire the resources you need, how could you improvise? What activities could you create to make your learners feel they are in employment? What health and safety/environmental factors must you take into consideration?

You may need to liaise with others in your organisation when setting up a RWE or contact external companies to see if they would be willing to donate anything, for example, equipment, or offer advice and support. If you can't obtain up-to-date equipment or new technology, you could arrange visits to companies to observe it in use. You could find out if your organisation would be willing to receive sponsorship money from organisations in return for publicity. Some employers are keen to be involved with RWE initiatives and will give their time to come in and talk to your learners. Others are happy to act as a potential employer for mock job interviews (possibly at their own premises or via a webcam) or even offer work experience in their organisation. When setting up the RWE do ensure you follow all organisational and legislative guidelines. You may need to add some aspects to the induction process or display relevant guidelines, for example, posters on walls.

You may have learners who will start and finish your programme at different times. Your organisation might offer a *roll on/roll off* system where learners can commence and complete at a time to suit them. This reflects the workplace, where staff may start or leave their employment at different points in their career path. You will need to create an individual induction to ensure all relevant aspects are covered, and make learners feel welcome by introducing and integrating them to the group. You could plan to deliver the theoretical topics on a rolling programme, perhaps covering one topic per month to ensure all learners can participate.

You may have a *learning support practitioner* attending some of your sessions to support a particular learner's needs. If so, ensure you brief them regarding the session, perhaps giving them a copy of your session plan in advance. During the session, make sure that you engage and involve them, as they will be there in a support capacity for learners and may not be competent with the topic you are delivering.

Ways to help create a productive RWE environment include:

- adopting a caring attitude;

- avoiding discriminating practices;

- being honest and realistic;

- being sensitive to the language (verbal and body) you use so that learners are not inadvertently offended;

- contextualising activities to the vocational area;

- creating challenging, interesting and engaging activities;

- having a positive and enthusiastic attitude;

- not dismissing learners' comments or suggestions as unhelpful;

- not having favourite learners to whom you allocate the best jobs;

- reinforcing learning through relevant activities;

- reviewing progress and praising achievements regularly;

- showing respect for each learner's individuality, culture and past experiences;

- treating your learners as individuals rather than as a group of people who are all the same.

Making your sessions realistic and challenging will help develop your learners' thinking and practical skills. This should increase motivation and hopefully improve achievement, enhancing the learning experience in the process. If you can also create links for work experience, this should enhance your learners' opportunities to gain employment. According to the Incomes Data Services survey, *Pay and Progression for Graduates* (2005), which questioned 96 employers, over a third (37.4%) of learners who had a work placement went on to obtain a position with the employer they had their placement with. The equivalent figure for those who took a holiday job was even higher at 47%. A work placement not only gives valuable experience, leading to the acquisition of new skills and knowledge, but enables a learner to gain a foot in the door towards employment.

Behaviour and motivation

The type of working environment you are trying to create should influence the behaviour of your learners. Wherever possible, you need to emphasise the importance of workplace ethics and try to model the behaviour that you expect from your learners. You should communicate, act and present yourself in an appropriate manner for the setting. If you behave in a manner which is suitable, it will help set an example for your learners, creating positive attitudes and values.

You may experience behaviour problems with your learners which could lead to disruption amongst the group. Creating an environment where your learners are self-motivated, challenged and stimulated to learn will help. If your learners are interested in the tasks they are performing, which are relevant to the vocational area in which they wish to work, this should maintain motivation. If disruptive situations do arise, ensure you deal with them immediately; otherwise this could lead to further disruption.

Learners may have issues or problems which they bring to your sessions, for example, immaturity, arriving late, talking amongst themselves, sending text messages or just appearing uninterested. Finding effective ways of dealing with disruption as it occurs will lead to an effective learning environment; however, this will mainly come from experiencing the situations and finding suitable strategies for yourself. Setting ground rules or having a group contract will help establish boundaries. Empowering your learners to take ownership of these should help ensure they are followed, leading to limited disruption.

Activity

Think about situations which have arisen during your sessions which have led to problems with behaviour. How did you deal with them? Did you deal with them immediately or choose to ignore them hoping they would go away? What would you do differently next time a similar situation occurred?

If you are passionate about your subject, this should help enthuse and motivate your learners. Keep your sessions active, involve your learners and build their self-esteem, ask relevant questions, use eye contact, use their names and give positive ongoing praise and feedback. Any subject can be made interesting to your learners; it is all about the way you choose to deliver it. A session is only boring to your learners if it is delivered in a boring way. If you are not interested, or do not prepare the activities adequately, your learners will not have confidence in you, leading to a lack of motivation, and possible disruption as a result. Setting positive expectations of your learners and encouraging them to accomplish tasks, even if this is in small stages, will help them see their progress and achievement.

People often behave in different ways depending upon the situation. Transactional analysis is a method of analysing communications between people as well as being a theory of psychological development. Eric Berne (1910–1970) studied personalities and the roles people take on. He argued that verbal communication, particularly face to face, is at the centre of human social relationships and psychoanalysis. The starting point is when two people encounter each other – one of them will speak to the other, this is known as a *transaction stimulus*. The reaction from the other person is known as the *transaction response*. The events and feelings that people have experienced are stored within them, and can be re-experienced in current situations. Berne (1964) identified three personality states; the *child*, the *parent* and the *adult* and argued that people behave and exist in a mixture of these states, due to their past experiences. Transactions are the verbal exchanges between two people: one speaks and the other responds. If the conversation is complementary, for example, adult to adult, then the transactions enable the conversation to continue. If the transactions are crossed, for example, adult to child, the conversation may change its nature or come to an end.

Transactions become crossed when people take on different roles in different situations. The best state for both parties to be in is the adult.

Example

Laura arrives late to Keith's session, delaying an activity which she had a significant part in. Keith could respond in one of three ways:

Parent – *'It's very inconsiderate of you to arrive late, the whole group has been kept waiting.'*

Child – *'See what you've done now? We're going to have to rush the activity or be late finishing.'*

Adult – *'Laura, I'd appreciate it if you could let me know next time you are going to be late, I can then make other arrangements.'*

When in the child state, you might feel small, afraid, undervalued, demotivated and rebellious. These feelings could make you undermine, withdraw, gossip, procrastinate, or attempt to please in order to be rewarded. In this state, you are not acting professionally.

Sometimes, you may find yourself acting like a parent to your learners. You may have learned your actions from your parents' responses to things you did years ago. You might feel superior, detached and impatient. Being in this state can make you harden your tone, not listen, begin to shout, bribe for compliance or criticise more than appreciate.

When you feel your child about to take over, you can choose instead to participate, find out the facts and resolve your differences. When you feel your parent about to take over, you can choose to speak warmly, be patient, listen and enjoy the challenge. It is very difficult to always be in the adult state. People change and adapt to different situations, and often respond to the states that other people they are with have taken on. However, the adult state is the best to be in for a successful outcome. As an adult, you feel good about yourself, respectful of the talents and lives of others, delighted with challenges, proud of accomplishments, and expectant of success. These feelings help you respond to your learners by appreciating and listening to them, using respectful tones, perceiving the facts, considering alternatives, having a long-term view, and enjoying work and life.

Berne (ibid) recognised that people need *stroking*. Strokes are acts of recognition which one person gives to another. This can be physical, or praise with words of appreciation which can be positive or negative. You will have opportunities with your learners to give positive verbal strokes which should act as a motivator and help build their confidence. Personal motivation can lead to positive behaviour, a good atmosphere and the achievement of tasks. Learners need to be self-motivated for personal reasons, such as earning a salary or gaining a promotion. They also need to be motivated by external factors such as helping the organisation achieve its objectives or targets. Being motivated at work should lead to improved behaviour, job satisfaction for the individual and a job well done for the organisation.

You can help create a motivated learning environment that is realistic by:

- asking learners what motivates them and planning activities around their interests, providing they are relevant;

- being democratic rather than dictating;

- celebrating achievements with awards ceremonies;

- challenging and stretching higher-level learners further;

- confronting any issues straight away, not ignoring problems thinking they will go away;

- encouraging healthy competition between groups;

- encouraging autonomy, initiative and responsibility;

- engaging learners in decision making;

- enriching the learning experience by offering opportunities for further development, for example, ICT training;

- expecting high achievement;

- following up any absenteeism and offering relevant support if necessary;

- generating a positive and comfortable environment;

- inviting feedback for the benefit of improvements;

- listening to your learners;

- promoting positive body language, and eye contact;

- recognising individual differences;

- rewarding good work with positive feedback;

- setting realistic tasks and targets that learners are keen to achieve;

- setting a good example yourself, for example dress, behaviour, respect;

- supporting lower-level learners, perhaps pairing them with a higher-level learner;

- taking an interest in your learners;

- trusting learners to work on their own initiative;

- using persuasion to encourage self-motivation;

- varying tasks and activities to alleviate boredom or routine.

You may be familiar with Maslow's (1954) Hierarchy of Needs which has five levels of needs ranging from warmth, shelter and food at the lowest level to realising self potential at the highest level. If you can make sure your learners' lowest level needs are met by providing a comfortable working environment with access to refreshments, they should be able to progress further. If a learner is hungry or cold, they may be thinking about this rather than their work.

Figure 4.1 Maslow's (1954) Hierarcy of Needs from an educational perspective

Creating a stimulating and challenging environment, which engages learners in relevant activities, will help promote positive behaviour.

Dress and personal presentation

There are often pre-conceptions of what appropriate dress should be for a given situation, as well as stereotyped images of what people look like from different countries or cultures. Stereotyping can lead to social categorisation and give negative impressions of people. For example, a nurse is often perceived as female and a doctor as male. A stereotype is a fixed, commonly-held notion or image, which is possibly wrong. These ideas might not be formed by an individual, but by external influences from others. You may need to challenge your learners' ideas, as it might be that what some learners feel is acceptable, others might not. There are situations when the dress code could vary; for example, some organisations have a *dress down Friday* where employees can wear something casual one day a week. Some organisations don't mind their employees working in casual clothes when not in contact with clients or the public. Others require professional wear at all times, or supply a uniform to signify a corporate image.

Activity

Design and use an activity with your learners to challenge any preconceptions or stereotypical images they have of what they consider is and isn't acceptable. This could then lead to the group agreeing an acceptable dress code for their learning environment.

Appropriate dress and behaviour in the learning environment should simulate what is acceptable in employment. It should influence the success of your delivery and ultimately the employability of your learners. If you are delivering in a motor vehicle workshop, it would be appropriate to wear overalls; in a training office smart clothes would be suitable. You could discuss different types of dress with your learners and look at pictures of people in different job roles and from different cultures. You could create an activity for lower-level learners to match a picture of a job role to the appropriate dress and then discuss what is acceptable and what isn't. You never get a second chance to create a first impression; the image you portray can influence how your learners choose to dress. Your organisation might have funding to supply specialised clothing to your learners if necessary, as some may not be able to afford their own. When your learners attend a job interview, they will need to present themselves well to create a positive first impression and portray the fact they are taking it seriously.

Aspects of personal presentation include:

- appearance;
- attitude;
- being fit and healthy;
- being optimistic and positive;
- body language;
- confidence;
- dress;
- minimal or no display of tatooes or excessive jewellery;
- paying attention to personal cleanliness and hair;
- personal and dental hygiene;
- personality;
- posture;
- self esteem and morale;
- speech.

If a learner takes pride in their appearance and presents themselves in a positive manner, they will give a good impression to a prospective employer. A learner's self confidence and self esteem may affect the way they present themselves. Previous situations and experiences may have influenced the way they are now. You may need to help learners gain the confidence and self-esteem they need to feel able to apply for employment.

Example

One of Ravi's learners, Abby, was quite shy and wouldn't take part in interview role plays. Ravi encouraged her to be one of the three interviewers, giving her one question to ask at an appropriate moment during the interview. On the next occasion, Ravi encouraged her to be one of two interviewers and to devise a question of her own to ask. On a third occasion Abby felt able to be the only interviewer and afterwards offered to play the role of the interviewee. Ravi had therefore built up her confidence gradually and as a result noticed she was more communicative during other activities.

Group activities such as role play can help, as well as taking learners out of their comfort zone, for example, asking them to give a presentation to their peers. The way you and other learners give subsequent feedback should be carefully managed so as not to demoralise.

You may have to be tactful with some learners who might not accept they need to make improvements, for example, with personal hygiene or cleanliness. Asking your learners to research personal presentation aspects they feel employers look for could be a way of helping them realise what is expected of themselves. Using visiting speakers and group discussions are useful ways of discussing sensitive topics in the open. Alternatively, you may need to have a one-to-one talk with a learner who might not be able to see they need help. Some learners may need strategies to deal with personal issues, for example, stress or time management. There may be colleagues in your organisation who could help, or you might need to refer your learners to a specialist agency. Always maintain confidentiality, respect and trust when communicating with others about your learners.

How your learners present themselves will have an impact upon their future careers. Giving consideration to these aspects when delivering employability programmes should help your learners appreciate the importance of personal presentation.

Summary

In this chapter you have learnt about:

- the training/realistic working environment;
- behaviour and motivation;
- dress and personal presentation.

References and further information

Ashley, R (2006) *Improving your employability*. London: Hodder Education.

Berne, E (1964) *Games people play – the psychology of human relationships*. London: Penguin Books.

Gravells, A and Susan, S (2009) *Equality and diversity in the lifelong learning sector*. Exeter: Learning Matters.

Heller, R (1998) *Motivating people*. London: Dorling Kindersley.

Hind, DWG (2005) *Employability skills*. Houghton-le-Spring: Business Education Publishers.

Incomes Data Services (2005) *Pay and progression for graduates*. London: IDS.

Wallace, S (2007) *Managing behaviour in the lifelong learning sector* (2nd edn) Exeter: Learning Matters.

Websites

Equality and Diversity Forum – www.edf.org.uk

Health and Safety Executive – www.hse.gov.uk

Maslow – www.maslow.com

5 REFLECTING THE NEEDS OF THE WORKPLACE

Introduction

In this chapter you will learn about:

- workplace requirements;
- group contracts;
- rewards and penalties.

There are activities and examples to help you reflect on the above which will assist your understanding of the needs of the workplace.

This chapter contributes towards the following scope (S), knowledge (K) and practice (P) aspects of the LLUK professional standards (A–F domains) for teachers, tutors and trainers in the Lifelong Learning Sector:

ASI, AS2, AS3, AS5;
AKI.I, AK2.I, AK2.2, AK4.I, AK4.2, AK5.I;
API.I, AP2.I, AP2.2, AP3.I, AP4.I, AP5.I, AP6.2;
BSI, BS2, BS3, BS4, BS5;
BKI.I, BKI.2, BKI.3, BK2.2, BK2.3, BK2.5, BK2.7, BK3.I, BK3.4; BK4.I, BK5.I;
BPI.I, BPI.2, BPI.3, BP2.I, BP2.2, BP2.3, BP2.4, BP2.5, BP3.I, BP4.I;
CS2, CS4;
CKI.2, CK2.I, CK3.I, CK3.2;
CPI.2, CP2.I, CP3.I, CP3.2, CP4.2;
DSI, DS2;
DKI.I, DKI.2, DKI.3, DK2.I;
DPI.I, DPI.2, DPI.3, DP2.I;
FSI, FS2, FS3;
FK3.I, FK4.I, FK4.2;
FPI.2, FP2.I, FP3.I.

The standards can be accessed at:
www.lluk.org.uk/documents/professional_standards_for_itts_020107.pdf

Workplace requirements

Your aim should be to create independent learners who will be able to obtain and sustain suitable employment and be competent and confident. Employers will want to retain skilled and knowledgeable people; training new staff can be expensive. The different working sectors of public, private and voluntary will have different workplace requirements and competition for jobs is high, particularly in an economic downturn. Working is an essential part of society and for some learners the working environment may be new, strange and possibly intimidating. Some learners, for example, school leavers or graduates may have little or no prior experience of work. Learners will need to understand the requirements of the workplace in general, as well as for the specific area within which they wish to work. They also need to know there is no guarantee of a job and they may have to change their career aspirations or put them on hold for a while. The following topics, which reflect aspects of the workplace, might be useful to integrate into your delivery:

- citizenship;
- organisation values and mission statements;
- contracts of employment;
- cultures and values within organisations;
- different payment methods of wages/salaries, for example, cash, direct debit;
- different working practices such as self-employment, franchise, remote and home working, flexi-time, etc.;
- disciplinary and grievance procedures;
- duties to be performed;
- equality and diversity;
- employee roles and responsibilities;
- employment legislation;
- health and safety;
- how to communicate, dress and interact with others;
- jargon and technical terms;
- knowledge of business, organisational brand and image;
- managing change and conflict;
- pensions, healthcare, shares, benefits and incentives offered by employers;
- relevant codes of practice, regulations and guidelines;
- the requirements for Criminal Records Bureau (CRB) checks;
- trade unions;
- training opportunities, appraisals and supervision;
- salaries and wages, i.e. how they will be paid;
- working with mentors;
- workplace environments and ethics.

You can help your learners appreciate what is required in the workplace by discussing these points for each of the sectors. Learners could research an organisation they would like to work for, find out as much as they can, and then give a short presentation to their peers. This would help improve their confidence, communication and presentation skills, as well as finding out useful information.

Activity

Research the differences between employment within the public, private and voluntary sectors. Make a list of a few companies in each sector, along with examples of roles and responsibilities for a particular job in each. You could then ask your learners to carry out a similar activity and compare and contrast their findings. This could lead to a discussion about workplace requirements, ethics and acceptable behaviour. You could take your learners to visit an organisation, increasing your own knowledge at the same time as theirs.

Learners may lack confidence and be nervous of entering employment if it is for the first time, after a period of unemployment, a career break, or a redundancy. Different jobs and workplaces will have different demands, for example, shift work, standing for long periods, working under pressure, being interrupted, commuting and/or long hours. You might be training staff who are currently employed but are facing unemployment. You will not only need to help these staff plan their future, but also those staff remaining within the organisation, for example, helping them with succession planning to cover the duties of those leaving.

Whilst learners are with you, they should behave in the manner to that which would be expected in the workplace. This includes:

- being on time;
- being organised and efficient;
- dealing with challenges;
- following health and safety aspects;
- following rules and regulations;
- dressing appropriately;
- maintaining self motivation and commitment;
- maintaining the right attitude and behaviour;
- not abusing break times;
- respecting others.

If you can create a learning environment similar to the workplace, this will help your learners deal with challenges and situations as they arise. In turn, this will help with their confidence and the realisation of a work-life balance. If you have learners who have experience of employment, you could create discussion groups whereby they could share their experiences with the others. Some may have carried out voluntary work, had a work placement or attended a club or association and could talk about these. Real experiences of how they felt when they first started, how other people treated them, the routines and rules they had to follow, what they had to wear and how they had to act will help your learners appreciate what is required in different contexts. Learners may have experienced unfamiliar feelings and emotions at work until they found their comfort zone. Finding out who to refer to for help, or how to obtain resources can be stressful in a strange environment. Some workplaces don't give a thorough induction or any training and expect the employee to get straight to work. Having a mentor or a buddy at work can stop feelings of isolation, but not all organisations offer this. This can leave people feeling isolated and lead to poor job satisfaction, ultimately leading to poor job performance.

There are times in the workplace when employees have to carry out tasks they don't want to do, or have to wear specialist clothing they don't like. You will need to make it clear to your learners that some of the tasks you ask them to do, need to be done, whether they want to do them or not. If you have a mixed group of learners with some having had employment experience, you could hold a discussion about aspects of work that your learners have enjoyed, or haven't, and how they dealt with it.

Employees should always be professional and work to the expectations of their employer whether full time, part time or temporary, earning the minimum wage or a high salary. Any personal problems should be left behind; the employer will want value for their money and not want timewasters. Some jobs offer a small salary and then a commission based upon job performance, for example, sales of a product or service. Learners will need to realise they can't just turn up at the workplace and get paid for attending, they need to be productive not complacent, and portray a positive attitude towards others and their job. You might have learners who have no idea how to behave when starting a job, or have their own expectations of what the employer should do for them rather than what they should do for their employer. You could carry out a group activity to discuss their expectations and their past experiences.

Prior to starting work, learners should plan:

- how to deal with any personal or family commitments beforehand;
- where they are going and what time they need to be there;
- what to wear – first impressions are important;
- what questions they need to ask such as who is their supervisor;
- their travel route;
- what they need to take, for example, a notepad and pen, tools, a packed lunch etc.

Using case studies and role play activities could help your learners understand various topics relating to workplace requirements, for example, teamworking, decision making, behaviour and problem solving. Learners will also need to know that they might make mistakes when they start work, and that they must admit to these. Otherwise, if they are found out, they may receive a warning or lose their job. Making a mistake is not failure – it is part of the learning process. Being honest and trustworthy will help gain the respect of colleagues.

Some workplaces may adopt an informal approach to working practices and communication between colleagues, whereas others might be quite formal. Learners will need to be aware of how to act in various situations, for example, being assertive rather than being aggressive or passive. You could ask your learners to find out the differences and role play various scenarios to see how they react.

If you have previous learners who have gained suitable employment, they may be willing to come in to talk to your current learners, or even mentor a learner. This could provide opportunities to share knowledge of the local labour market and the expectations of employers. Encouraging learners to get in touch with local employers could lead to work placements and offers the opportunity for making contacts and networking.

Example

Antonio, a 24 year old learner who had recently become unemployed, had decided he wanted to become a carpenter. He had gained some experience at school and made items as a hobby. His teacher set him a project to research local companies who employ carpenters and encouraged him to write a letter to ask if there was the possibility of visiting the organisation to have a look around. One organisation replied and asked him to get in touch. Antonio telephoned the organisation and arranged a visit date. The director who showed him around was very impressed with his enthusiasm and asked him if he would like to gain some work experience. This gave Antonio a chance to gain valuable skills and knowledge and to realise he did want a career as a carpenter. The work experience then led to a part-time paid position.

You might be delivering employability programmes within an organisation to help reduce staff turnover and retain good employees. Investing in new staff can be expensive in terms of training and lost productivity; investing in current staff can lead to a motivated workforce and improvements in productivity. Tamkin and Hillage (1999) in their report *Employability and employers: the missing piece of the jigsaw* stated employers should develop a comprehensive policy towards employability. If you are working with an employer for the benefit of their employees, you need to:

● be clear why employability is felt to be a desirable initiative;

● explore when job transitions may be likely and who would be affected;

● consider the organisation's financial circumstances, the skills of the workforce and the external labour market conditions;

● decide which aspects of employability are likely to be the most important;

- develop processes that will enhance those aspects of employability judged to be most useful;

- communicate the organisation's commitment to employees;

- sell the approach to line managers and individuals;

- clarify roles and responsibilities – who needs to do what? What is the role of the individual?

- monitor and evaluate the approach taken.

Finding out what employers expect from their employees will help your learners appreciate what is expected of them, whether they are aiming to sustain their current employment, or gain employment in the future.

Group contracts

Creating and agreeing a group contract with your learners will help ensure your sessions run smoothly and encourage all learners to behave in an acceptable manner. You might already set ground rules with your learners which can form part of the contract. The group contract can be used just like a contract of employment, enabling learners to understand what is expected of them along with their roles and responsibilities. You might already agree a type of contract with your learners, such as an individual learning plan (ILP), which will outline the qualification/s to be achieved. A group contract is more about behaviours and attitudes. When you start with a new group of learners, or new learners join an existing group, you should discuss and agree the rules that everyone should abide by. These could include:

- arriving on time;

- attending regularly and informing you of any absences with the reason why;

- dressing and behaving appropriately;

- meeting deadlines to enable tasks to be achieved;

- no eating or drinking;

- no swearing;

- respecting others;

- switching off mobile phones and music players.

Incorporating the rules into a group contract can help set the boundaries for everyone and create a working atmosphere which reflects the needs of the workplace. The group contract should be written in language and terminology that all learners understand, and be applicable to the environment, for example, formal sessions or a realistic working environment (RWE). Any individual needs should also be taken into consideration when creating the contract. Your organisation might have a standard contract for all learners to sign, or you could agree separate contracts with each group of learners you have. The latter would introduce the concept of negotiation and agreement. Some funding bodies require a contract to be signed and qualifications to be achieved before releasing any money. If learners are involved in the setting of the ground rules and a group contract, they should take ownership and responsibility for them. If a learner doesn't follow them, other learners might reprimand them before you need to.

Continued implementation of the group contract is important to maintain structure and order; there may be penalties imposed upon learners if the contract is broken.

Example

At the beginning of the programme Rick explained the purpose of the group contract along with penalties, and agreed the ground rules. These were then typed up, signed by all learners and displayed on the wall. When a learner left their mobile phone on, other learners would reprimand them reminding them of the rules. One learner, Jack, consistently arrived late and was given verbal warnings. Most of the learners knew that after three verbal warnings a written warning would be given. They knew that in employment a dismissal would then follow. This was pointed out to Jack and he then made the effort to be on time.

You might like to carry out a group discussion, with your learners listing the *dos* and *don'ts* that they feel are acceptable in the workplace. A visiting speaker could be invited to attend, who would add currency and vocational relevance. The resulting lists could be turned into a group contract which all learners sign. This could be placed on the wall of the room for all to see, and/or copies given to each learner. If a new learner joins the group, they should be given a copy of the contract and included in any revisions. Referring to the contract regularly will keep learners focused on the requirements. The contract could be revised or updated at appropriate times in the programme to suit any changes in circumstances.

When negotiating with your learners, you might encounter barriers that each individual may have. You may have learners who have never used a computer before, or have difficulty writing or spelling; you may have learners who have English as a second language, or who are apprehensive about attending interviews. Learners may lack confidence due to past experiences such as a redundancy or periods of unemployment. Others may be nervous of starting a first job or changing career. You will need to help your learners overcome any barriers by being supportive and/or referring them to others for specialist advice.

Your learners will need to function as part of a team, both during your sessions and in the workplace. Teams can evolve naturally, but understanding the stages of team development may ease some of the difficulties that can be encountered. Individuals often act differently depending upon the situation and the other people they are with at the time. How you act towards your learners may also be different depending upon the context or circumstances you are delivering in. Different issues will arise when delivering to individuals, as opposed to groups. When delivering to a group, accept that this is a collection of individuals, all with different needs and wants, and that it is up to you to address these whilst keeping focused on the topic of learning.

Belbin (1993, p24) defined team roles as: *a tendency to behave, contribute and interrelate with others in a particular way.* His research identified nine clusters of behaviour, each of which is termed a *team-role*. Each team-role has a combination of strengths they contribute to the team, and allowable weaknesses. See the table on page 73.

The team-roles are grouped into *action*, *people* and *cerebral* roles:

- *action-oriented* roles: Shaper, Implementer, and Completer Finisher;

- *people-oriented* roles: Co-ordinator, Teamworker and Resource Investigator;

- *cerebral* roles: Plant, Monitor Evaluator and Specialist.

Sometimes teams become problematic, not because their members don't know their subject, but because they have problems accepting, adjusting and communicating with each other as they take on different roles. You might like to carry out a group activity with your learners to see how they take on these different roles. Knowing that individuals within teams are different will help you manage group work more effectively. For example, you could have a mixture of *action*, *people* and *cerebral* roles within each group.

Coverdale (1977) states that the essence of team working is that individuals have their own preferred ways of achieving a task, but that in a team, they need to decide on one way of achieving this. In a team, three needs have to be focused upon at all times: the *task needs*; *the team needs*; and the *individual needs*.

To achieve the task effectively, you will need to ensure that:

- aims and objectives are stated;

- responsibilities are defined;

- working conditions are suitable;

- supervision is available.

To build and maintain the team you will need to ensure that:

- the size of the team is suitable for the task;

- health and safety factors are considered;

- consultation takes place;

- discipline and order are maintained.

To develop the individual you will need to ensure that:

- responsibilities are defined;

- grievances are dealt with;

- praise is given;

- learners feel safe and secure.

Belbin® Team-Role Summary Descriptions

Team-Role Descriptions

Team Role	Contribution	Allowable Weakness
Plant	Creative, imaginative, unorthodox. Solves difficult problems.	Ignores incidentals. Too pre-occupied to communicate effectively.
Resource Investigator	Extrovert, enthusiastic, communicative. Explores opportunities. Develops contacts.	Over-optimistic. Loses interest once initial enthusiasm has passed.
Co-ordinator	Mature, confident, a good chairperson. Clarifies goals, promotes decision-making, delegates well.	Can be seen as manipulative. Offloads personal work.
Shaper	Challenging, dynamic, thrives on pressure. The drive and courage to overcome obstacles.	Prone to provocation. Offends people's feelings.
Monitor Evaluator	Sober, strategic and discerning. Sees all options. Judges accurately.	Lacks drive and ability to inspire others.
Teamworker	Co-operative, mild, perceptive and diplomatic. Listens, builds, averts friction.	Indecisive in crunch situations.
Implementer	Disciplined, reliable, conservative and efficient. Turns ideas into practical actions.	Somewhat inflexible. Slow to respond to new possibilities.
Completer Finisher	Painstaking, conscientious, anxious. Searches out errors and omissions. Delivers on time.	Inclined to worry unduly. Reluctant to delegate.
Specialist	Single-minded, self-starting, dedicated. Provides knowledge and skills in rare supply.	Contributes on only a narrow front. Dwells on technicalities.

Bruce Tuckman (1965, 1975) identified five stages in the process of group development: a four-stage model was published in 1965 and a fifth stage added in 1975. These are:

- forming;

- storming;

- norming;

- performing;

- mourning aka adjourning.

Forming – this is the *getting to know you* part. Group members may be anxious and need to know the boundaries and codes of conduct, for example, 'What shall we do?'

Storming – this is where conflict can arise, such as rebellion against the leader, resistance to the tasks and disagreements, for example, 'It can't be done!'

Norming – this is where group cohesion takes place and the norms are established for the group. Mutual support is offered, views are exchanged and the group co-operates, for example, 'It can be done'.

Performing – individuals feel safe enough to express opinions. There is energy and enthusiasm towards the task, for example, 'We are doing it!'

Mourning – the task is complete and the group separates. Members often leave the group with the desire to meet again or keep in touch, for example, 'We will do it again!'

Most groups will progress through these five stages; however, some may not go through all of them, or even jump backwards or forwards. This shows that groups take time to form and work together effectively.

Activity

Create a scenario for a role play that you could use with your learners to help them work as a team. This could include situations that will test their negotiation and communication skills. Observe the activity and see how your learners interact with each other and how focused they remain. See how they take on different roles and compare these to the theorists' models.

Group discussions and role play can help learners to act out situations to gain experience of dealing with conflict. Conflict between individuals will inevitably happen at some time or other. Helping your learners to handle conflict successfully will enable them to learn from their experiences and strengthen the way they communicate.

Setting and agreeing ground rules and having a group contract can help learners follow the expectations of the workplace.

Rewards and penalties

Some employers offer rewards for their staff who perform well, for example a financial bonus or retail vouchers. This can be seen as an incentive to perform well. Penalties or sanctions may be imposed upon staff who do not perform well or break the rules. Rewards and penalties can be used to motivate staff, but they can also demotivate. Employees who do not gain rewards may be jealous of those who do; conversely they might be motivated to do better. Using rewards and penalties during your sessions can demonstrate the positive benefits of working well, or the consequences if not. If you wish to reward your learners you will need to find out if your organisation is supportive of this and if a budget is available. You will also need to ask yourself whether you feel it is right to give rewards for things that should be expected as the norm. You may be working in an organisation that does not, or cannot, provide money for, or agree with giving rewards. Giving praise and encouragement can be an excellent reward, and of course is free. You could carry out a discussion with your learners to agree if rewards should be given and if so, what they will be.

Rewards could be given for:

- adding extra value or *going the extra mile* with a task;

- completing work ahead of target dates;

- excellent performance or 100% attendance;

- significant and outstanding achievements;

- teams that have worked exceptionally well together.

Rewards could include:

- access to leisure facilities;

- an award ceremony;

- external visits to organisations;

- fun activities and competitions;

- praise and encouragement;

- retail vouchers;

- in-house certificates of merit;

- points or tokens which can be redeemed at the end of the programme for a gift or trophy;

- promotion to a supervisor role in a RWE;

- refreshments;

- *thank you* or *well done* cards.

Giving rewards can be a motivator and an incentive to work harder. However, learners should be performing to their best ability as a matter of course. Rewarding the good behaviour of a learner who is usually the opposite might work well for that particular learner, but what about those who are consistently working well? It might be useful to keep a record of what you give and to whom, to ensure you are being fair to all learners within your group. Try and praise the ongoing effort your learners are making, rather than just what they have achieved. This should help maximise the effort they put into a task and encourage them to see the benefit of the work they carry out rather than just the completed outcome. Praise doesn't cost anything, whereas other rewards might prove expensive to your organisation. Job satisfaction can be a self-reward. If you can encourage your learners to take pride in what they are doing, and give ongoing praise and encouragement, this would alleviate the need for rewards that could be seen as bribery. Setting examples to your learners, such as arriving early, keeping the room tidy and having a positive attitude should help create a culture that your learners will emulate.

Hopefully, having agreements in place early on in the programme should alleviate any problems that occur. However, there will be times when you need to give a penalty or sanction to your learners. Not doing so would demonstrate to your learners that it is all right for them to get away with something, and soon you would have disorder in your session. You could carry out an activity with your learners to agree what the consequences will be for certain situations.

Penalties could be given for:

- arriving late;
- bad attitude;
- breaking the ground rules;
- breaking the group agreement;
- inappropriate actions;
- inconsistent attendance;
- non-completion of tasks;
- not bringing the required tools or equipment;
- not listening to or following instructions;
- not wearing the required clothing;
- not working in a safe manner;
- poor behaviour;
- refusing to work.

Penalties/sanctions could include:

- a reduced break time;
- a reduction in training allowance;
- additional tasks/homework to be completed by a set time/date;

- being asked to leave the programme for very serious matters;
- being closely supervised;
- cleaning or tidying the environment;
- having to work on their own;
- losing access to the internet;
- reduced access to facilities;
- verbal and written warnings.

When giving sanctions your message needs to be simple, clear and not negotiable, and you also need to be consistent. Don't get into a confrontational situation or argument with your learner. If possible, move into a position whereby you can be at the same eye level. This ensures you are not leaning over them in a dominant way. Standing or sitting side by side with them is more likely to gain their attention. If they have done something wrong, they need to realise this, accept the consequences and move on. Be discreet, try not to embarrass your learner in front of their peers, and be specific. Once you have delivered your sanction, check your learner has understood and then continue with your session. Your learner may retaliate and try to defend their position or try to create an argument with you. Keep calm, repeat what you have said, then move away and continue with your session. No one likes receiving a sanction, particularly in front of their peers, therefore the longer the interaction between you both, the more chance an argument may arise. Remain professional and make sure your learner abides by your requests. You may have to give another sanction if your learner doesn't follow the first one. By doing this, you are showing the other learners they cannot get away with something. Sometimes you might not need to give a sanction, but just prompt your learners.

Example

Amy had a group of learners in the beauty RWE. She noticed Helen and Gavin hadn't submitted today's project by the agreed time of 4 pm and that they were both now looking at a website. She went over to them, pulled up a chair and sat down beside them. She said firmly, 'I needed you to submit your project on time, can you tell me what the delay is?' Helen then explained they had been researching a particular website for some further information. Gavin added that he should have informed Amy of the delay. Amy then said, 'That's fine, do keep me informed in future if you can't meet a deadline. I'll be back in ten minutes to check on your progress.'

This example shows that Amy is monitoring what is going on, has stated what she expects of her learners and will keep a check on them. If the project wasn't then completed, a sanction could be given whereby Helen and Gavin would have to stay late to complete it.

Your tone of voice, body language or the look on your face can gain attention and show you are in charge. An assertive manner, rather than an aggressive manner, whilst keeping to the facts should help your learners realise what is expected. Don't get personal – you might not get along with some of your learners but this is no reason to show them up in front of their peers or give sanctions without a genuine reason. All learners need to know the boundaries within which they are expected to work; they also need to know the consequences if they do not follow the rules or break their contract.

Activity

What rewards and penalties could you use with your group, to reflect the requirements of the workplace? Think of instances when you would give a reward or a penalty and how you would do it.

The demographics of the country are continually changing. The *veteran* generation (aged 55 plus) may have been with the same employer for a long time and be thinking of retiring, have probably paid off their mortgage, have children who have left home and therefore have different priorities to the other generations. The *baby boomers* (aged 46–54) might be working fewer hours and increasing their leisure pursuits, have grown-up children and a low mortgage. This generation will increase over the next few years, leading to a greater number of older than younger people in the job market. *Generation X* (aged 30–45) might be mid-career, have had several jobs, and perhaps have experienced redundancy and unemployment along the way. They might have a large mortgage and a growing family. *Generation Y* (aged 18–29) will be first or second jobbers, might still be living with their parents, have few responsibilities and might have a large debt. They use technology a great deal and the line between work and social use can become blurred. With these different generations come different aspirations, expectations, attitudes and values towards work. You may have mixed groups of learners from the different generations who have experienced these differences first hand.

Tamm Communications, a top 100 Canadian employer, state there are ten different workplace differences between Generations X and Y:

1. Preferred style of leadership:
   - **X** – only competent leaders will do;
   - **Y** – collaboration with management is expected.

2. Value of experience:
   - **X** – don't tell me where you have been, show me what you know;
   - **Y** – experience is irrelevant, as the world is changing so fast.

3. Autonomy:
   - **X** – give them direction, and then leave them to it;
   - **Y** – questions, questions, questions.

4. Feedback:
   - **X** – expect regular feedback;
   - **Y** – need constant and immediate feedback.

5. Rewards:
   - **X** – freedom is the ultimate reward;
   - **Y** – money talks.

6. Training:
   - **X** – want to learn continually, if they don't they will leave;
   - **Y** – still in an exam-driven mentality.

7. Work hours:
   - **X** – do their work and go home;
   - **Y** – will work as long as needed ... or until they get bored.

8. Work life balance:
   - **X** – they want to enjoy life to the full, while they are young enough to do so;
   - **Y** – their lives are busy – they need a lot of *me* time.

9. Loyalty:
   - **X** – they are as committed as everyone else working there;
   - **Y** – already working out their exit strategy.

10. Meaning of money:
    - **X** – it gives freedom and independence;
    - **Y** – just something that allows them to maintain their lifestyle.

One of the greatest differences between Generation X and Y seems to be what they want from work. Generation X is enticed by freedom and independence and get on with their jobs without asking too many questions. Generation Y is more money and lifestyle oriented, focused on their own interests and used to 24 hour access to products and services. Another difference between the two generations relates to the use of technology. Generation Y have been brought up with technology and see it as embedded in, and integral to their life. They have had the opportunity to use the internet, e-mail and various computer programs at school and expect to be able to access all of these at home and at work. They embrace new technology with ease, expect instant access to information, use social network sites, and don't often have independent thought or retain information as it is so easy to locate. They have a *what's in it for me* attitude and often expect a reward for doing something for someone. To them, their social life comes first. Generation X, in contrast, mainly use technology for convenience, for example, online banking and shopping but it tends not to play much of a part in their social lives. A new generation is now growing up known as *Generation Z* (or the *i-generation* meaning the internet generation). They have had lifelong access to technology, the internet and communication tools such as instant messaging, blogs, text messages, twittering, online videos and social networking. Access to multimedia to such an extent can lead to a change in communication methods which can lead to a lack of social manners. Communication can become wholly technology-based rather than face to face and can lead to poor spelling and grammar. Personal aspects often take priority over work due to the *immediate* and *switched on* lives they lead. The opposite may also occur such as the desire to check work e-mails in their own time. This generation has been subjected to a fame culture through the many reality television shows and is often influenced by celebrities and fashion. However, an economic downturn may lead to a change in this generation's attitudes, for example, they tend to have increased concern for the environment; they are often not being as indulgent as their parents were, and tend to recycle and reuse products more consistently.

The availability of jobs for the various generations will differ. School leavers and graduates may struggle to get a job without having had relevant experience. Older people, although very experienced, may not have the technological skills required. Being aware of this will help you understand the different aspirations, expectations, attitudes and values of the generations, particularly if you have different age ranges within the same group.

Summary

In this chapter you have learnt about:

- workplace requirements;
- group contracts;
- rewards and penalties.

References and further information

Belbin, M (1993) *Team roles at work*. Oxford: Elsevier Science and Technology.
Coverdale, R (1977) *Risk thinking*. Bradford: The Coverdale Organisation.
Gravells, A and Simpson, S (2009) *Equality and diversity in the lifelong learning sector*. Exeter: Learning Matters.
Tamkin, P and Hillage, J (1999) *Employability and employers: the missing piece of the jigsaw*. Report 361, Institute for Employment Studies.

Websites

Generation X and Y – www.personneltoday.com
Tamm Communications – www.tcicanada.com
Tuckman – www.infed.org/thinkers/tuckman.htm

Introduction

In this chapter you will learn about:

- reflective practice;
- personal development;
- continuing professional development.

There are activities and examples to help you reflect on the above which will assist your understanding of reflective practice, and how to determine personal and organisational development needs.

This chapter contributes towards the following scope (S), knowledge (K) and practice (P) aspects of the LLUK professional standards (A–F domains) for teachers, tutors and trainers in the Lifelong Learning Sector:

AS4, AS6, AS7;
AK4.I, AK4.2, AK4.3, AK6.I, AK6.2;
AP3.I, AP4.I, AP4.2, AP4.3, AP6.I, AP7.2, AP7.3;
BK2.6;
BP2.6, BP2.7, BP3.4;
CSI, CS3, CS4;
CKI.I, CKI.2, CK4.I, CK4.2;
CPI.I, CP3.4, CP4.I;
DS3;
DK3.I, DK3.2;
DP3.I, DP3.2;
EKI.2, EK2.4, EK4.2;
FS3;
FK3.I.

The standards can be accessed at:
www.lluk.org.uk/documents/professional_standards_for_itts_020107.pdf

Reflective practice

It is important to reflect upon your delivery and working practices, to enable you to think about what you have done, how you did it and why you decided to do it in a certain way. This will enable you to change or improve your practice in the future.

All reflection should lead to an improvement in practice, for example, you may feel you work well as a member of a team, but your colleagues might think differently. There are many theories regarding reflective practice, some of which will be explained within this section. Others have been covered in the companion book *Planning and enabling learning* by Gravells and Simpson (2008).

A straightforward method of reflection is to have the *experience*, then *describe it*, *analyse it* and *revise it* (EDAR). This method should help you think about what has happened and then consider ways of changing and/or improving it.

EDAR: **Experience** → **Describe** → **Analyse** → **Revise**

(Gravells, 2008)

- *Experience* – a significant event or incident you would like to change or improve.

- *Describe* – aspects such as *who* was involved, *what* happened, *when* it happened and *where* it happened.

- *Analyse* – consider the experience deeper and ask yourself *how* it happened and *why* it happened.

- *Revise* – think about *how* you would do it differently if it happened again and then try this out if you have the opportunity.

A way of getting into the habit of reflective practice is to complete an ongoing journal. However, try not to write it like a diary with a description of events, but use EDAR to reflect upon and analyse the event. See Appendix 8 for a journal proforma.

Reflections don't always have to be written – often, when you finish delivering, you will be thinking about your delivery, perhaps on your journey home. You might discuss it with a colleague in the staff room and find they have had similar experiences to yours. Discussions with others can enhance your own experiences, although it is important to maintain confidentiality if you are talking about specific learners. At some stage, you will be observed by an inspector, verifier, supervisor, colleague or mentor. Their feedback will enable you to reflect upon your delivery with a view to making improvements. You may need to learn how to accept constructive criticism and feedback from others. Don't take any criticism personally, it's probably not you, but the situation that might need changing.

Reflection should become a part of your everyday activity and will enable you to look at things in detail in a way that you perhaps would not ordinarily do. There may be events you would not want to change or improve as you felt they went well. If this is the case, reflect as to *why* they went well and use these methods in future sessions. If you are not able to write a reflective journal, mentally run through the EDAR points in your head when you have time. As you become more experienced at reflective practice, you will see how you can make improvements.

Brookfield (1995) identified the importance of being critical when reflecting. He advocated four *points of view* when looking at practice which he called *critical lenses*.

These lenses are from the point of view of:

1. the teacher;
2. the learner;
3. colleagues;
4. theories and literature.

Using these points makes the reflection *critical*. Firstly, look at it from your own point of view, and then secondly look at how your learner perceived your actions and what they liked and disliked. Thirdly, take the view from colleagues, for example, taking a mentor into consideration. This enables you to have a critical conversation about your actions which might highlight things you hadn't considered. Fourthly, you should link your reflections to theories and literature, comparing your own ideas to others.

Example

Julia, a trainee teacher, came away from a one-to-one training session feeling it hadn't gone well. From her point of view, George, the learner, hadn't been paying attention. Julia tried to analyse why this was and came to the conclusion he was acting this way because she was being observed by her mentor. Afterwards, Julia asked him why he hadn't been paying attention. To her surprise, he responded by saying the work wasn't challenging him enough. Julia's mentor felt the same as the learner, as he could see George had appeared bored. This helped Julia realise she needed to broaden George's learning experiences further. She could relate this to Schön's (1983) theory of reflection in action/reflection on action. Next time, Julia will be able to reflect immediately she realises a problem (in action), rather than waiting until afterwards (on action).

Reflection can be facilitated by a *critical friend* who is willing to question, challenge and offer sympathetic support and advice to overcome issues or problems. You could pair up with a colleague to challenge, question and support each other. This support can be useful in establishing actions to overcome barriers. Critical friends can be used to engage in conversation or to review each other's reflective writing. In the latter case, the critical friend would read your journal entries and make written comments which should challenge your thinking. This should then promote a positive change in your reflective practice.

Johns (2006) uses guided questions in his model for structured reflection. The questions are posed and answers are written in a reflective diary. *Cue questions* focus on the experience, for example, the *here and now* of the experience, the causes of the experience, the context/background to the experience and the key processes related to this experience. The subsequent questions focus on *what* was the purpose of the actions, feelings and consequences for all involved. The *influencing factors* are then explored, for example, what influenced the decision making. The final question is *could I have dealt better with the situation?* This explores the choices available that led to the situation. Using this method will help you understand the influencing factors behind your subsequent actions.

Formats for maintaining journals or writing about incidents use headings to generate thought processes, for example, Gibbs's (1988) reflective cycle. The headings prompt you to consider aspects such as:

- What happened?

- What was I feeling at the time?

- What could I have done differently?

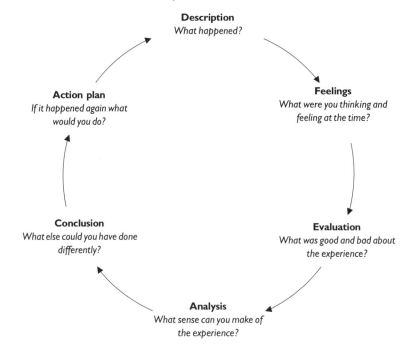

Figure 6.1. Gibbs's reflective cycle (Gibbs, 1998)

Activity

Work through Gibbs's (1988) reflective cycle for a recent session you have delivered (see Figure 6.1). Compare your findings to another reflective model, for example, Brookfield (1995) or Johns (2006).

Reflection is a form of self-evaluation. Evaluating your delivery and other aspects such as learner attendance, retention and achievement will help you reflect holistically upon your role. Ways of evaluating your delivery include questionnaires, online surveys, verbal feedback, results from tests and assessments, etc. Information gained from evaluations must lead to improvements for your learners, yourself and your organisation. Never assume everything is going well just because you think it is.

Other ways of evaluating your programme include obtaining feedback from:

● colleagues;

● employers;

● inspectors;

● managers;

● mentors;

● staff from partner organisations such as the Youth Service, Connexions, etc.;

● verifiers and moderators from awarding bodies;

● workplace supervisors.

Programme evaluations ensure learning has been successful (or not) and inform future planning. If your programme hasn't been successful, i.e. several learners either left or didn't achieve the qualification, your organisation might decide not to offer the programme again. Retention and achievement rates can affect the amount of funding received to offer a programme.

Your own reflective practice, along with learner and programme evaluations will ensure you continually improve your delivery and the service your learners receive.

Personal development

Feedback from others, for example, observations of your delivery, can help you reflect on and evaluate your role. This should help you identify areas for your personal development and give you ideas to improve or modify your practice. Your organisation may require you to keep a Personal Development Plan (PDP) with short, medium and long term aims and targets. This will ensure you are continually updating your practice and the service you give your learners. You might need to plan and organise relevant activities yourself, or this might form part of an appraisal system within your organisation. Whilst you might be knowledgeable and experienced regarding your subject, you might not be so good with aspects such as literacy, numeracy and ICT. Taking a positive approach to your personal updating will ensure you improve your own skills and knowledge to support your learners. However, if your organisation is funding your development, you will need to ensure anything you do fulfils their needs as well as your own.

Activity

Talk to your mentor or a colleague and obtain feedback regarding your personal development. Based on this feedback, and your own reflections, complete the personal development plan in Appendix 6.

Setting yourself targets for your personal development, and keeping to these, will help you remain skilled and qualified in an ever-changing sector/marketplace. If you don't have a mentor, you could ask a colleague to act as one. Mentors are experienced professionals, in your own subject area, who can give you advice and support.

> *Mentoring is to support and encourage people to manage their own learning, in order that they may maximise their potential, develop their skills, improve their performance and become the person they want to be.*
>
> (Eric Parsloe, The Oxford School of Coaching and Mentoring www.theocm.co.uk)

Having a mentor brings many benefits. For example, you can gain:

- access to different experiences and activities;

- access to resources;

- advice and support based upon personal experiences;

- an impartial listener who will challenge your potential;

- detailed constructive and developmental feedback;

- introductions to useful people at work and beyond;

- knowledge and expertise about your organisation and sector;

- motivation, encouragement and guidance.

You should be proactive in keeping up to date with your own skills, the needs of employers generally, and in specific sectors and organisations. The skills required to gain and sustain employment and to progress within a chosen career are subject to continuous change. You will want your learners to achieve a relevant qualification and obtain suitable employment therefore your own abilities, skills and knowledge should accurately reflect the workplace and its practices. If you have hobbies, interests, a part-time job, or belong to various clubs or societies, you could refer to these during your sessions and relate various anecdotes to your learners. It could be that you have worked in industry and have lots of experience you can draw on to pass on to your learners. If you don't have any industrial experience, you might consider carrying out some relevant work to complement/improve your delivery. Learners will respect the fact you have *been there and done that* and should feel able to ask questions about the world of work, which you can reliably answer.

Example

Joseph had worked in an office as an administrator since leaving school. He gained a Business Administration qualification on the job, and certificates in Information Technology at evening classes. Over the years, he progressed to supervisor level and delivered various staff training sessions. Due to organisational cutbacks last year, Joseph's position was restructured to a part-time role. After achieving the Preparing to Teach Award, he decided to teach one day a week, which enabled him to pass on his skills and knowledge to others. He felt confident at answering all the questions from his learners, as he had experience in the world of work. He was also able to draw on these experiences to plan and deliver interesting and relevant sessions.

Your own personal development will need to take into account the context of delivering employability skills. For example, you might have experience of working in an office, but not in the different contexts of employment, for example retail, manufacturing or local government. You will need to consider how you can develop yourself in many other areas to increase your knowledge.

The employability and economic climates are constantly changing; therefore you need to consider ways of keeping up to date, to limit the impact of changes and developments upon yourself and your learners. Your knowledge of the subject and of best practice in planning, delivering, mentoring, supporting, training, and assessing should remain current, as well as taking into account any national and/or legislative developments. Many awarding bodies require you to be competent and confident to a level above that which you will be delivering and assessing. For example, if you are delivering a Level 2 qualification, you should be competent and confident at Level 3.

You may feel you are quite confident and capable with all aspects of your subject delivery, knowledge and skills. However, there are always opportunities for further learning to increase these. Eraut and Hirsh (1998) link workplace learning with performance and capability.

> *Capability is obviously influenced by learning but also current capability influences the ability to learn. Capability is required by job performance but is also developed through job performance. The context in which the individual is working and learning influences how their capabilities are perceived, how they perform and how they learn. An individual can be seen as highly effective in one setting and not another. Individuals are in a dynamic relationship with their work setting, being both influenced by it and being part of it themselves and through their relationship with others.*

> (Eraut and Hirsh, 1998, p7)

You will find your own capability changing as you develop both personally and professionally. You might feel you are quite capable at the moment in all aspects of your job, but at what level do you consider yourself to be? This is not a qualification level, but the level of your own performance. Dreyfus and Dreyfus (1986) advocate a model of progression to explain the process by which people gain experience when learning a new skill, which leads to proficiency. The model has five levels and shows that people pass through different levels as they become more experienced. Each level has different characteristics, for example, at the early levels people don't want lots of theory and can't tolerate ambiguity. They want to be told specifically what to do to achieve a goal, and they want to see lots of short-term successes. However, as experience is gained, needs change. For example, you start needing to put information into a broader context, and to applying it in your own way. You will become less rule based, and more intuitive. Table 6.1 on page 88 gives examples of these.

The ways in which an absolute beginner becomes a novice are different to what will help a proficient person move on to being an expert. Novices use basic rules, and often struggle with working out how best to apply the rules to a given situation. Competent people benefit from simulations that help them further develop their application techniques. Proficient people learn best through case studies. Experts learn through their experience, and still continue to learn and develop their understanding, often using a strong sense of intuition gained through their experience. Looking at the table you might find you are at different levels for different activities. Knowing this will help you identify areas for development and help you create situations where you can learn in a more appropriate way.

Table 6.1. A model of progression
(Dreyfus and Dreyfus, 1986, cited in Eraut, 1994, p124)

Level 1	Novice	• rigid adherence to taught rules or plans; • little situational perception; • no discretionary judgement.
Level 2	Advanced beginner	• guidelines for action are based on attributes or aspects (aspects are global characteristics of situations that can be recognised only after some prior experience); • situational perception is still limited; • all attributes and aspects are treated separately and given equal importance.
Level 3	Competent	• coping with crowdedness; • now sees actions at least partially in terms of longer-term goals; • conscious deliberate planning; • standardised and routine procedures.
Level 4	Proficient	• sees situations holistically rather than in terms of aspects; • sees what is most important in a situation; • perceives deviations from the normal pattern; • decision-making is less laboured; • uses maxims for guidance, whose meaning varies according to the situation (a maxim is a brief expression of a simple truth, a code of conduct).
Level 5	Expert	• no longer relies on rules, guidelines or maxims; • intuitive grasp of situations based on deep tacit understanding; • analytic approaches are only used in novel situations or when a problem occurs; • vision of what is possible.

The Dreyfus model advocates that as mastery in a skill is gained, there is an increase in the ability to apply abstract rules to concrete situations.

Peter (1969) argued that people are promoted to their highest level of competence, after which further promotion raises them to a level just beyond this and they become incompetent. This has become known as the *Peter Principle*:

> *In time, every post tends to be occupied by an employee who is incompetent to carry out his duties . . . work is accomplished by those employees who have not yet reached their level of incompetence.*

> (Peter, 1969, p138)

In an organisation's hierarchy, staff may be promoted as long as they work competently. However, sooner or later they may be promoted to a position at which they are no longer operating competently and they will remain there, operating incompetently and unable to gain further promotions.

It could be that you feel quite comfortable with your job role at the moment, but if you are promoted, you might not be able to carry out your new role as effectively as you thought. Although sometimes it is good to move out of your comfort zone and embrace new challenges, you may be placed in situations where you do not have the necessary skills or knowledge to deal with them effectively.

Peter's (ibid) levels of competence are:

1. **unconscious incompetence** – you don't know how to do something, but don't know that you don't know this. To reach the next level, you need to know *what* it is that you don't know;
2. **conscious incompetence** – you know what you want to do, and start to appreciate the gap in your competence. To reach the next level you need to know *how* to become competent;
3. **conscious competence** – you can do what you set out to do, but have to give it a lot of attention. Through repeated practice you can reach the next level;
4. **unconscious competence** – you can perform a skill easily without giving it a great deal of thought. Once you achieve unconscious competence, you are at a level which suits your ability at the time.

Being aware of your personal development and your confidence and competence at performing your job role, will help you plan areas for your further improvement and advancement.

Continuing professional development

There are constant changes in education, therefore it is crucial to keep up to date with any developments. Examples include changes to the qualifications you will deliver, changes to policies and practice within your organisation, regulatory requirements and government policies. Your organisation may have a strategy for continuing professional development (CPD) which will prioritise activities they consider are important to improving standards. CPD can be formal or informal, planned well in advance or be opportunistic, but should have a real impact upon your job role, leading to an improvement in practice to benefit your learners.

If you are working towards Associate or Qualified Teacher Status in the Learning and Skills Sector (ATLS/QTLS), you must evidence your CPD annually. Once you have achieved your ATLS or QTLS status, you will need to maintain your licence to practice by partaking in relevant CPD activities, which the Institute for Learning (IfL) will monitor and sample. You also need to abide by their Code of Professional Practice.

Opportunities for professional development include:

- attending events and courses;
- attending meetings;

- e-learning activities;

- evaluating feedback from peers and learners;

- improving your own skills such as ICT;

- membership of professional associations or committees;

- observing colleagues;

- researching developments or changes to the subject and/or relevant legislation;

- secondments;

- self-reflecting;

- shadowing colleagues;

- standardisation activities;

- studying for relevant qualifications;

- subscribing to and reading relevant journals;

- taking the qualification yourself;

- visits to other organisations and work experience placements;

- voluntary work;

- writing or reviewing books and articles.

All CPD activities must be documented in some way and reflected upon. This can be via the IfL website, your organisation's own systems, or a manual/electronic CPD record.

Example

Refer to your personal development plan completed in a previous activity in this chapter (Appendix 6). Review the activities completed so far and complete the CPD record in Appendix 7, or upload your activities and reflections to the IfL Reflect website (www.ifl.ac.uk/cpd.reflect).

Always keep a copy of any documentation relating to your training and CPD, as you may need to provide this to funding, awarding, professional or regulatory bodies if requested. Maintaining your CPD will ensure you are not only competent at your job role, but also proficient. Being proficient will come from experience over time, and of dealing with real situations, issues and problems.

The difference between being competent and being proficient can be compared to a trained worker and an experienced worker. The experienced worker will normally be more productive, need less supervision, be more aware of contextual variations and be competent in a wider range of situations. Such changes involve unlearning as well as relearning, and a return to being a novice without the excuse of being a novice. Hence the need for time and support is an order of magnitude greater than that normally provided.

(Eraut, 2004, p14)

The ability to manage change comes with experience and knowledge. Charles Darwin (1809–1882) stated *it is not the strongest species that survive, nor the most intelligent, but the ones who are most responsive to change.* Change is a regular occurrence within education, and within employment. The pressure for change could come from the government, from regulatory bodies or from within your own organisation. Whatever the change, it will be inevitable it will take place; therefore you need to embrace it, communicate any concerns and ensure you find out the facts to move forward with it. Fear of the unknown may make you apprehensive and worried. Don't be anxious or become stressed if you are unsure of anything. The best way to embrace change is to look towards the future and the benefits the change will bring. Whilst you might not agree with the changes, they are being brought in to improve or amend a situation for a particular reason and all staff should be committed towards them. If your job role will change substantially, make sure you are fully aware of what these changes are and how you are expected to implement them. Being unsure of how changes will affect you personally and professionally can cause resentment towards others. Never be afraid to ask questions to clarify any concerns you have. Being positive about change and moving forward with your organisation can lead to new experiences, rewards and job satisfaction.

Force field analysis is a management technique developed by Lewin (1951) to help understand change processes. It is useful for planning and implementing change and attempting to overcome resistance to change. Lewin (ibid) assumes that in any situation there are both *driving* and *restraining* forces that influence any changes that may occur. Driving forces are those which affect a situation and push it in a particular direction; they can be negative or positive, for example, incentives for meeting targets met. Restraining forces are those which act to hold back or decrease the driving forces, and are often negative, for example, apathy or fear of failure. Equilibrium is reached when the sum of the driving forces equals the sum of the restraining forces. However, this equilibrium can be affected by subsequent changes in the relationship between the driving and the restraining forces.

Using a diagrammatic approach can help generate a force field analysis (see Figure 6.2 for an example). The driving forces and restraining forces are identified with arrows to denote different strengths, indicating how weak or strong they are.

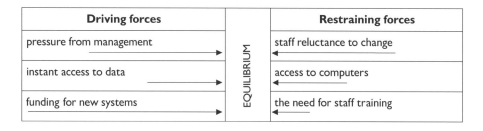

Figure 6.2 Force field analysis for the introduction of an electronic register system

To achieve change, three steps should be followed:

- the organisation must amend the driving and restraining forces that hold it in its current state;

- an imbalance should be introduced to the forces to enable the change to take place. This can be achieved by increasing the driving forces and reducing the restraining forces, or both;

- when the change is complete the forces are brought back into an equilibrium and a new current state is achieved.

If you embrace change and maintain your personal and professional development, you should see an improvement in your practice, resulting in a positive impact upon your learners' progress and achievement.

Summary

In this chapter you have learnt about:

- reflective practice;

- personal development;

- continuing professional development.

References and further information

Brookfield, SD (1995) *Becoming a critically reflective teacher.* San Francisco: Jossey Bass.

Dreyfus, HL and Dreyfus, SE (1986) *Mind over machine: the power of human intuition and expertise in the era of the computer.* Oxford: Basil Blackwell.

Eraut, M (1994) *Developing Professional Knowledge and Competence.* London: Falmer Press.

Eraut, M (2004) Learning to change and/or changing to learn. *Learning in Health and Social Care,* 3 (3): 111–17.

Eraut, M and Hirsh, W (1998) *The significance of workplace learning for individuals, groups and organisations.* Oxford and Cardiff: Economic and Social Research Council.

Gibbs, G (1988) *Learning by doing: a guide to teaching and learning methods.* Oxford: Further Education Unit.

Gravells, A and Simpson, S (2008) *Planning and enabling learning in the lifelong learning sector.* Exeter: Learning Matters.

Hitching, J (2008) *Maintaining your licence to practise.* Exeter: Learning Matters.

Johns, C (2006) *Engaging reflection in practice: a narrative approach.* Oxford: Blackwell Publishing.

Lewin, K (1951) *Field theory in social science.* New York: Harper and Row.

Peter, LJ and Hull, R (1969) *The Peter Principle: why things always go wrong.* New York: William Morrow and Company.

Roffey-Barentsen, J and Malthouse, R (2009) *Reflective practice in the lifelong learning sector.* Exeter: Learning Matters.

Schön, D (1983) *The reflective practitioner.* London: Temple Smith.

Websites

Charles Darwin – http://darwin-online.org.uk/

Institute for Learning – www.ifl.ac.uk

Managing Change – *How to manage change in an organisation*: www.oursouthwest.com/SusBus/mggchange.pdf

Oxford School of Coaching and Mentoring – www.mentorset.org.uk/pages/mentoring.htm www.theocm.co.uk

Post Compulsory Education and Training Network – www.pcet.net

7 SAMPLE ACTIVITIES TO CARRY OUT WITH LEARNERS

This chapter contains activities which you may like to use with your learners to increase their confidence, skills and knowledge. They are examples only, and can be adapted to suit your learners' requirements, qualification and level. They will require access to computers and the internet; however, you can easily adapt them if you have other suitable resources such as books and journals available.

When using the activities, you need to ensure they are inclusive, and differentiate for individual learning styles and needs, learner difficulties and/or disabilities. Make sure your learners are aware why they are carrying out the activities and how they relate to their qualification and employment in general. Supervision and support is required to enable successful and meaningful achievement.

After each activity, carry out a debrief with your learners either individually or in groups. Consider what went well and what you would change or improve for your next group of learners.

The activities listed below are also available from the publisher's website: www.learningmatters.co.uk

1. SWOT analysis (strengths, weaknesses, opportunities, threats)

2. Skills analysis

3. Gantt chart

4. Preparing for employment

5. Hypothetical job application and interview

6. Networking

7. Teamworking and communication

1. SWOT analysis

Complete a SWOT analysis to list your strengths and weaknesses along with the opportunities and threats to obtaining employment. When complete, consider how you can use your strengths to obtain employment and how you can turn your weaknesses into strengths. Act on the opportunities and try and turn the threats into situations to help you succeed. Searching the internet for *SWOT analysis* will locate examples and templates. An example is given below.

strengths	weaknesses
• a good timekeeper, honest, reliable • excellent communication skills	• have difficulty using a computer
opportunities	**threats**
• could turn my hobby of gardening into a business	• experienced competitors

2. Skills analysis

Make a list of the skills you feel you possess and those you need to develop. State how you can prove you have demonstrated the skills or how you could develop them for the future. Searching the internet for *skills analysis* or *employment skills* will locate examples. An example is given below.

Skills	How I achieved/How I can achieve
problem solving enthusiasm confidence communication	In my last job I noticed some forms we had to use were taking too long to fill in. I persuaded my supervisor to try a different approach and the revised forms were then used by the whole team, resulting in savings in time.
computer skills	I need to achieve a suitable qualification by attending a training programme.

3. Gantt chart

Prepare a Gantt chart; this is a visual tool to enable you to plan ahead, for example, to gain employment. First of all, make a list of the activities you need to do to obtain suitable employment. Secondly, consider how long it will take you to achieve each one. Produce a chart to map your activities; in the example below, you can see how some overlap. Searching the internet for *Gantt chart* will locate ideas and templates. An example is given below for one week.

1st Feb	2nd Feb	3rd Feb	4th Feb	5th Feb	6th Feb	7th Feb
research labour market and organisations (online, telephone and in person)						
	prepare cv					
complete SWOT analysis						
	list skills and areas for develop-ment					
		write and send spec letters				
		obtain and complete application forms				
				practise interview technique with friend		

4. Preparing for employment

- Research the labour market and organisations you would like to work for. You can do this via the internet or by telephoning/visiting organisations and recruitment agencies. An online search for *recruitment* will bring up lots of job sites. Consider the results of your SWOT and skills analysis to help you decide where you would like to work. Speak to people already in the job role to find out about any jargon they use, or special requirements that the organisation expects of employees. Look at the organisation's website to gain knowledge.

- Prepare a curriculum vitae (CV). Search the internet for *preparing a CV* to obtain ideas and templates. Check carefully for presentation and spelling errors.

- Write letters to the organisations you would like to work for, to ascertain if they have any suitable positions, or if they will keep your CV on file. Search the internet for *writing spec letters for jobs* to obtain ideas.

- Obtain application forms and complete these carefully, following all instructions. You may need to refer to your CV for the dates of qualifications, achievements and experience. Some may be completed online so be careful of your spelling and grammar. Always keep a copy of what you have written in case you are asked about it during an interview, and always be truthful.

5. Hypothetical application and interview

- In a small group, write a job advert, a job description, a list of essential and desirable skills required, and design and produce an application form.

- Display the advert and ask learners from the other groups to apply for the job by a certain date/time. They will then complete and submit the application form by referring to the job details.

- Have a discussion in your group to agree an appropriate number of shortlisted applicants who will then be interviewed. Plan dates/times for interviews.

- Role play the interviews in a proficient and serious manner. One person from your team can interview or you could have a panel of interviewers. The interviewee should have planned well, have some pre-prepared questions ready to ask, and act professionally throughout.

- After the interview, discuss and appoint a suitable applicant and tell them why they were successful.

- Give feedback to those that were not shortlisted or were not selected for interview.

This activity could be taken further by inviting local employers to carry out mock interviews for hypothetical jobs at their organisations. Alternatively, good and bad role plays can be demonstrated by your learners.

6. Networking

- Research the type of organisation you would like to work for and find out all you can about them. This can be by looking at their website or talking to people who currently work there.

- Write a letter to see if you can obtain voluntary or temporary employment, or to ask if they have any apprenticeship opportunities. If you do gain a placement, get to know as many people as you can while you are there and learn as much as you can. Be enthusiastic, keen to help and professional at all times. Maintain a diary and update your CV with your newly acquired skills and experience. When the time comes to leave, ask if you can keep in touch and keep a list of names and contacts. Send an occasional polite e-mail to keep in touch. Write a thank you letter afterwards – you might have made such a good impression that they will get in touch with you when a job does arise.

- Use the internet as an opportunity to network with others through social networking sites, twitters, blogs, etc. Always remain professional and never post anything that could give a negative impression of yourself.

- Attend meetings and events. Large organisations welcome non-employees to get involved with meetings, social gatherings and organising promotional events. You might not be paid, but you could make some useful contacts. Your local library, Jobcentre Plus, training providers or recruitment agencies may have open evenings and events you could attend. This would enable you to meet possible employers, find out about work experience, training and apprenticeships.

- Join community groups, youth centres, churches, sports clubs, charities, etc. to meet people and make contacts. This way you are doing something useful and rewarding whilst you are looking for employment.

- Keep a list of all your contacts and their details – an address book is useful or obtain business cards. If you say you are going to keep in touch with someone, make sure you do, as this keeps your name fresh in their memory in case a suitable job does come up.

7. Teamworking and communication

- In small groups, create a fictitious organisation. Discuss and agree a suitable name for the organisation and what they will offer, such as goods or services.

- Write a mission statement – you might like to research other companies' mission statements for ideas.

- Design a logo, a business card and an advertising leaflet or website using ICT.

- Produce a short presentation using multimedia if possible, to promote your organisation. You could have a special offer as part of the launch.

- Deliver your presentation to the rest of the group. You will need to decide whether all team members do this or just one.

- Obtain feedback from your peers to help you reflect on how you performed as an individual and as part of a group.

Delivering employability skills unit:
Level 4 (six credits)

Learning Outcomes The learner will:	Assessment Criteria The learner can:
1. Understand the difference between employability skills and employment skills.	1.1 Discuss the difference between employability skills and employment skills. 1.2 Review the advantages and disadvantages of each in the current marketplace/workplace.
2. Understand the personal qualities, skills and competencies needed for employability skills delivery.	2.1 Analyse the skills, qualities and competencies required for delivering employability skills and review own strengths and weaknesses in this context. 2.2 Demonstrate and evaluate interpersonal skills and a range of creative communication techniques appropriate to persuasive employability skills delivery. 2.3 Select, use and justify a range of constructive feedback techniques to underpin employability skills training.
3. Understand how to plan and deliver creative, innovative and inclusive sessions appropriate for employability skills delivery.	3.1 Explain and justify how the needs of target audiences should be taken into account when planning and preparing employability skills training sessions and support materials. 3.2 Identify and review the strengths and weaknesses of a range of training techniques and approaches to teaching employability skills to highlight the importance of creativity and innovation.
4. Understand how environment and personal presentation influence the success of employability skills training.	4.1 Employ and evaluate a range of strategies used to transform the training area to reflect a realistic working environment. 4.2 Employ and evaluate a range of strategies that challenge pre-conceptions of appropriate dress and behaviour.
5. Understand how to use group contracts, rewards and penalties to reflect the workplace.	5.1 Discuss the principles of the design of group contracts, justifying how they reflect the needs of the workplace. 5.2 Analyse ways of negotiating and defining behavioural parameters for employability training in the production of the group contract.
6. Understand the need for continuous personal development to reflect changing sector/marketplace requirements.	6.1 Explain, justify and use a proactive approach to personal updating and development which will reflect changing sector/marketplace requirements. 6.2 Use reflective practice and feedback from others to evaluate own role in delivering employability skills and identify areas for personal development, suggesting modifications to own practice.

The *New overarching professional standards for teachers, tutors and trainers in the lifelong learning sector* (LLUK, 2007) can be accessed at:
www.lluk.org.uk/documents/professional_standards_for_itts_020107.pdf, or by using the shortcut: http://tinyurl.com/5mmg9s

Tips for delivering employability skills

- Liaise with others, for example, to arrange work placements or to set up a realistic working environment (RWE).
- Ensure a suitable initial assessment is used with your learners before they commence, as this will help you plan your sessions based upon their knowledge/experience and needs. You can also arrange any necessary language, literacy, numeracy or ICT training.
- Consider how you will deliver the programme to suit the needs of the learners and the curriculum, and prepare a scheme of work. If you offer a rolling programme, ensure new learners are made welcome and integrated into the group.
- Prepare a thorough induction to include: learner responsibilities; centre responsibilities; requirements of the qualification; ground rules; group contracts and individual learning plans.
- Have starter activities available for your learners in case they can't all arrive at your session on time. This could be a quiz to recap learning so far.
- Devise innovative activities relevant to the syllabus and/or assessment criteria and level of your learners, for example practical tasks such as role play. Make your sessions as realistic as possible to workplace requirements.
- Encourage learners to complete a *work placement diary*. This will help them gain evidence towards relevant units and summarise their learning and experience (sample available in Appendix 3).
- Prepare your session plans in advance, ensuring that you cover the learning outcomes in an interesting and challenging way.
- Check the timings for your sessions are realistic. It is useful to have an extra activity prepared in case have spare time, or know what you can leave out if you run short of time.
- Prepare an accessible resource bank of information relating to employment and local organisations.
- Whenever possible, use activities with your learners which reflect the requirements of the workplace.
- Use visiting speakers from various organisations and specialist subject colleagues when possible to discuss current issues, skill shortages, personal and career development, etc.
- Have a contingency plan in case anything goes wrong or is not available.
- Arrive early to check the environment, set up and test equipment and resources, and ensure all learners can see and hear you.
- Introduce yourself, your topic and the aim of your session. It is useful to have your aim visible throughout your session.
- Deliver your topic confidently and ask questions regularly to check knowledge. Always use learners' names, and include all learners in the group.
- When speaking, use eye contact and stand tall, speak a little slower and louder than normal, and be aware of body language.
- Check all written resources for spelling/grammar/punctuation/syntax.
- When facilitating a group activity, think about what you will be doing whilst learners are active and ensure all learners participate.
- Prepare extension activities to challenge higher-level learners.
- Give regular feedback and encouragement to help motivation, try and appreciate what your learner is feeling based upon their experiences, for example, redundancy.
- Recap your aim in your summary and state what will be covered in the next session (if applicable).
- Evaluate yourself afterwards using reflective practice techniques.

Work placement diary

This section to be completed at the beginning:

Name:	
Work placement name and address:	
Work placement contact names and numbers/e-mail:	
Start date:	
End date:	

This section to be completed at the end:

Summary of activities carried out:	
Summary of skills, knowledge and personal qualities gained:	
Aspects for improvement/ development:	
Action plan – to obtain or sustain employment (CV to be created or updated):	

Date:	Activities carried out:	Skills/knowledge/personal qualities gained:	Action required:

Scheme of work

Teacher:			
Programme/Qualification:	Group:	Dates from:	to:
Number of sessions:	Contact hours: Non-contact hours:	Venue:	
Aim:			

Integrate functional skills of English, mathematics and ICT where possible and the themes of Every Child Matters

Consider differentiation, quality and diversity individual learning needs and learning styles

Dates:									

Session plan

Teacher:	Date:	Venue:
Subject and level/syllabus reference:	Time and duration:	Number of learners:
Aim of session:		
Group composition:		

Integrate functional skills of English, mathematics and ICT where possible and the themes of Every Child Matters

Consider differentiation, quality and diversity individual learning needs and learning styles

Timing:	Objectives or learning outcomes:	Resources:	Teacher activities:	Learner activities:	Assessment:

Personal development plan

Name:

Organisation:

Timescale:	Aims:	Costs involved/ Organisational support required:	Start date:	Review date:	Completion date: (CPD record to be updated)
Short term					
Medium term					
Long term					

Continuing professional development record

Name:	Organisation:			IfL number:	
Date:	Activity:	Venue:	Duration:	Justification towards role/Subject specialism:	Further training needs:	Evidence ref number: (e.g. personal reflections, notes, certificates, etc.)

Reflective learning journal

Name:	Date:

Experience *(significant event or incident)*	
Describe *(who, what, when, where)*	
Analyse *(why, how, impact on teaching and learning)*	
Revise *(changes and/or improvements required)*	

INDEX